HOLD

MW00795417

LETTING GO

A Memoir

By Heather Hutchison

.

The names and identifying characteristics of most individuals and places in this book have been changed to protect their anonymity.

ISBN 978-1-7753797-0-6 (Paperback)

Edited by Maraya Loza-Koxahn

Cover photo by Chelsea Dawn Photography

www.heather-hutchison.com

This book contains themes of suicide, mental illness, sexual and physical violence, and may be disturbing to some readers. If you need support, or are concerned about a loved one, please refer to the resources at the back of the book.

This book is not a substitute for medical or psychiatric care.

CONTENTS

Part II: Island General Hospital

PROLOGUE

I don't know when I first realized my life was optional, something I could hold in my own two hands and take away when I saw fit. As I lie awake in a darkened hospital room, I scan back through the years, searching for answers and reasons I may never fully understand.

Maybe it was exposure to mental illness and suicide at an early age, maybe it was when the problems at home started, or an inability—both learned and innate—to cope with stressful situations. Maybe it was because the school bullies told me I should kill myself. Or perhaps it was growing up faced with frequent discrimination caused by being born blind.

Realistically, it was probably a perfect storm of circumstances that came together with disastrous timing to lead me to this hospital bed.

PART I:
HOW DID THIS HAPPEN?

The Beginning

I remember the exact moment I knew that I'd forever be seen as different. Until a certain age, children don't appear to take much notice of differences in themselves or others. If they do happen to notice some difference, they don't seem to view it as anything more than a simple fact, neither positive nor negative. It is the people around us who teach us to judge and fear.

In my first few years of life, it never occurred to me that I was different. Like every young child, I idolized my older brother and cousins. I tagged along behind them like a pesky shadow as they wrestled with one another, raced each other on their bikes, built forts, and climbed trees. I was determined to do everything they did. Nobody ever told me I couldn't.

I was on summer vacation at the coast with my family when that all changed. Five years old, I played contentedly at the playground near our campsite with a boy who was a few years older than me. My hands and face were sticky with melted ice cream and summer heat. The only two children on the playground, we became fast friends, racing each other across the monkey bars and up and down the slides. When he asked me why I never looked at anything, I told him matter-of-factly, "I'm blind."

Suddenly and swiftly, he turned on me. As I stood at the top of the slide, he shoved me so hard I tumbled backwards, landing in a heap a few feet away, on the wooden platform that led to the slide.

"Blind bozo!" he yelled over his shoulder as he flew down the slide, jumped on his bike and peddled away as though the hounds of hell were on his tail, spewing playground sand in his wake.

I didn't move or cry out. I lay where I'd fallen on the smooth wooden planks of the playground structure, warm on my back from the afternoon sun. As I tilted my face up toward the sky, tears rolled silently down my cheeks. I already hurt in all the places where bruises would soon form. My young, as-of-yet unmarred body was also aching in places where the marks wouldn't show but would be carried for a lifetime. I cried not for the pain of the fall, but because with his words, a thousand little things clicked into place for me. I was, in fact, different from everyone else I knew; and different was bad. With stunning clarity in that moment, I understood I would forever be known as the girl who had something wrong with her. Forever is an awfully long time when you're five years old.

I made a silent promise to myself that day on the playground that I would find a way to keep my blindness a secret from everyone.

When I was only a few months old, my parents took me to the pediatrician. They were concerned that I wasn't focusing on the people and things in my environment as other babies did. Although it would take years to receive an actual diagnosis, doctors were quick to label me legally blind.

Blindness is not all or nothing; it is classified on a continuum. Through visual tests and, eventually, my own verbal descriptions of what I was seeing, my degree of vision was classified as "light perception" only; however, it was (and still is) more complicated than that. It quickly became obvious that my visual impairment was severe. Although I had a small amount of vision, there was no doubt I would be a braille reader, and that I would be unable to navigate in unfamiliar environments without the use of a cane or guide dog.

Although I spent more time than other children being poked and prodded in specialists' offices, I didn't give it any real consideration. I didn't understand, or care, when the doctors said I wasn't meeting some of my developmental milestones. At two years old, I was too young to understand my parents' grief when they received my official diagnosis of congenital blindness, or their fear for what my future may hold.

My mother wept as I lay sedated on the MRI table, looking impossibly small and fragile in my white hospital gown. All the eye charts I couldn't read surrounded us in the sterile examination rooms of so many specialists. Tears pricked behind my eyes as blood was drawn and sent to be studied in faraway laboratories to search for the cause of my blindness. Perhaps these vague memories are not actual memories at all; perhaps I only "remember" because I was told about them years later.

In fact, I remember my father's cancer diagnosis and hospitalization the summer I turned three better than I can recall any worries I may have had about my own disease. Smell being our most primal sense, it stuck with me—the antiseptic smell of sickness permeated my brain as I sat, quiet and bewildered on my father's hospital bed while he rested, and a heavy rain fell outside. This event reappears more readily than my own battery of tests.

The early childhood educators who came to our home to support my physical development were nothing more to me than adults who played fun games and did crafts with me. I basked in the extra attention. It never occurred to me that other children didn't need this level of support with learning to do things that required basic motor skills or hand-eye coordination. When I began to learn to read and write in both print and braille, I didn't stop to consider that other kids were only learning print. I had a mild curiosity about why other people saw things I couldn't, but it didn't frustrate me. Before that day on the playground, my blindness was simply part of who I was, no different than having brown hair and blue eyes.

My family members had a wide range of responses to my blindness while I was growing up. For some, it appeared all-consuming, something they needed to frequently talk about and explore. Eventual treatment options were a common topic of discussion. "One day, when there's a cure, we'll rent a giant hall and have a huge party with everyone you know," my parents would tell me. What, exactly, would there be to celebrate? It wasn't like getting "fixed" would be a great success I'd achieved on my own. It seemed like they thought I'd be a better version of myself if and when my blindness was cured.

Other family members sometimes tried to pretend my blindness didn't exist. "Just leave your cane in the car. We'll only be in the store for a minute," they'd say. "Can you put your cane away?" cousin Nate asked me once. "Everyone is staring at us." I always tried to give each family member what I thought they needed to feel better about my disability; because if they were comfortable, I would be comfortable too. Trying to balance these two extremes was exhausting and futile.

In elementary school, I pored through books, intently studying the words used to convey the body language of fictional characters, trying to understand how to respond to situations like a sighted person would. In my child's mind, I figured if I just tried harder no one would ever know. I wished my parents would fix me. If they could heal a skinned knee with a Band-Aid and a popsicle, why couldn't they make my eyes better?

In addition to blindness, I was diagnosed with Hypotonia, or floppy infant syndrome. I was born with low muscle tone, so did not have strong arm and leg movements or head control. This initially caused my neuro-ophthalmologist to hypothesize that potential cognitive impairment would need to be further investigated. As I began to reach cognitive milestones early, this theory was put to rest. As part of my physical therapy, I was enrolled in piano lessons in the first grade with the hope that playing piano would strengthen my hands and wrists and help with my fine motor skills.

Although music was an innate passion for me, I was a terrible student. The pieces in my books written by boring dead guys held little interest for me. Seated on a stack of phone books to reach the keys of the little upright in my childhood home, I listened to the steady ticking of the old-fashioned egg timer, willing it to ring, signalling my freedom. Sometimes I would shift the dial ahead ever so slightly, shaving minutes off the excruciating half hour of practice. The days I felt motivated to play, I got lost in the delight of composing my own music or interpreting songs I'd heard on the radio.

My first piano teacher was a no-nonsense, birdlike woman who always wore her steel-grey hair in a severe bun, and never seemed to smile. Nearing retirement, she had little patience for childish antics. She tutted about my lack of progress as I sat, week after week, at the Yamaha baby grand in the living room of her drab condominium, which smelled strongly of mildew and curry. Much to her probable relief, I did not stay in lessons for more than a few years. It was not, however, the end of music for me. Although I didn't know it at the time, the piano would eventually offer me a critical lifeline.

Despite the undeniable challenges of growing up in a society that was not designed for me to move through with grace, I had a full, rough-and-tumble childhood. It was filled with bike rides, water skiing and downhill skiing, ice skating, rollerblading, gymnastics, swimming, martial arts, music lessons, and school clubs. I had a solid group of friends and was close with my brother and cousins. Long summer days were spent running barefoot with my friends through our suburban neighbourhood with its big houses, tall trees and perfectly manicured lawns. We beat the summer heat by sliding through frigid sprinklers on a banana yellow Slip 'N Slide, and flew down the streets on scooters, skateboards and rollerblades. Icy Northern Canadian winters were punctuated by backyard hockey games and family ski trips to the mountains. I did not grow up in a protective bubble, as many children with disabilities unfortunately do. My parents allowed me the freedom to fall, and encouraged me to get back up and try again.

I loved nothing more than to be transported to other worlds, either by the books I read voraciously, or the stories, poems and songs I was constantly writing. Books in braille were a limited resource in the 90s; every single book I could get my hands on was a cherished possession. I learned to appreciate books from most genres, and books written for readers far beyond my level. I meticulously memorized entire chapters down to the exact words, and entertained family and friends with dramatizations of the stories I devoured.

As the years passed, creativity became my escape. I enjoyed being on the stage in any capacity, whether in school plays, talent shows or music recitals. I carried an old clunky tape recorder with me everywhere, dictating fantasy stories of wild adventures and singing made-up songs for hours. I was content to exist in my own little world. I dreamed of being a famous singer one day and made a deal with my older brother to loan me a hundred dollars, which, at six years old, I figured would be more than enough money to record my first album.

Although some of my childhood remains shrouded in darkness, most of my early years were happy.

First Signs

Over the years, I have tried to make sense of just how and when things went wrong for me. As a young child, I had been happy and extremely outgoing. I was the kind of kid who would chat away happily to people I'd just met as though they were longtime friends. As time passed and I gained more self-awareness, I began to withdraw. I had started to realize that some people seemed to be uncomfortable in my presence, and I spoke less and less to people outside of my immediate circle.

As I withdrew from the outside world, I became aware of my parents' increasing struggles. We lived in a shadow world; our blinds drawn against would-be thieves and predators that were undoubtedly lurking in our middle-class, suburban neighbourhood. Danger hid around every corner. Catastrophe was likely at any moment. Their struggle to maintain some semblance of control in a frightening, chaotic world exhausted them.

Lying in bed at night, I would listen to them yell about things I was far too young to understand. Then, one night when I was six, the yelling stopped. That night, my dad left quietly as I slept.

After living apart from us for a time, my father moved back home. But I had learned something during his absence. My parents' anxiety made a lot of sense to me.

Disaster could strike when you least expected it; you could fall asleep one night and, by the time you woke up next morning, one of the most important people in your life could be gone.

By the second grade, I had begun to struggle with severe anxiety around changes in routine or fear of being punished. In school, I would worry so much about doing something wrong and getting into trouble that I would get frequent severe stomach aches and have to be sent home early. Finally, my anxiety reached a point where I could no longer attend a friend's birthday party without becoming so anxious, I would throw up.

On my eighth birthday, I arrived home to a surprise party my mother had planned for me. As I came through the door, a dozen third graders sprang from their hiding places, screaming "Surprise!" at the top of their lungs. I immediately locked myself in the bathroom. Sinking down onto the closed lid of the toilet, I tried to breathe. I began to sweat, and waves of nausea rolled through me. My vision began to dim, and I felt like I was falling. I had not yet learned to recognize a panic attack, and had no idea what was happening to me. Eventually, I could breathe again, and my racing heart began to slow. I left the bathroom and joined my friends to sing karaoke, pretending everything was okay.

I also began to notice that I was slowing down my friends during some activities and I knew they were starting to realize it as well. When we'd go to an amusement park—a frequent pastime—I couldn't navigate the stairs and obstacles as quickly as they could. Inevitably, a friend would stay behind with me, ignoring the urge to run ahead to ride as many rides as possible. My close friends never said anything to me, but they didn't have to. I knew, and the knowing only worsened my anxiety.

I was intentionally excluded from certain activities. I was told that a friend's mom wouldn't allow me to come to my friend's birthday party because she didn't think their home was safe for blind people, whatever that meant. Another mother expressed concerns over me being a member of a babysitting club that my friends and I started; although I'd earned my babysitting certificate just like the rest of the girls, I mysteriously stopped hearing about club meetings.

Some of my classmates started to treat me differently. They would steal from me and move things I was using; they would disguise their voices, asking, "Who am I?"

"An idiot," I would answer wryly. This oh-so-original joke would then inevitably devolve into them waving their hands in front of my face and asking if I knew how many fingers they were holding up. "I don't know. How many am I holding up?" I'd answer, extending a middle finger in their direction. They usually got the point.

If I couldn't hide my blindness from others, my follow-up tactic was to educate them. By my own initiative, I began going to the classrooms of the particularly obnoxious kids to talk about my life as a blind person. I would read to them from my braille books, show them how my cane worked, write each of their names in braille, and answer a myriad of questions. It was intimidating, particularly visiting the older grades. Eventually, teachers from other classes, and even other schools, asked me to give presentations to their students.

The question periods at the end of my presentations could be challenging. Questions ranged from hilariously awkward, "How do you know when you're... you know... done wiping?" to perplexing, "If you don't see only darkness, what can you see?" The latter question was difficult to answer. If the shoe was on the other foot, how would a fully sighted person describe their vision to me?

"I can tell the difference between light and dark," I'd explain. "I can also recognize objects in low-light conditions. If the light is just right, I can, for example, identify the shape of a person, though I can't see enough to know who they are. If print letters on a piece of paper are several inches high, I can read a few words before my eyes get too tired to see anything at all. I might be able to tell that a colour is bright, but be unable to identify the actual colour, apart from red, which I can see in certain light. I can also see stark contrasts, such as someone with dark hair and light skin, or black and white checkered floor tiles. In bright light, I'm pretty much completely blind. I see best in dimly lit rooms, or in the brief twilight after sunset, before the sky is completely dark. How much I can see varies by the day; if I'm tired or stressed, my vision is worse than when I'm relaxed."

Unfortunately, education only helps those who want to learn; many of the biggest bullies weren't interested.

By my early teens, the innocent playground games had turned more sinister. My stomach in knots, I would sit in class, waiting for the lunch bell to ring and the bullying to begin. I became hard and angry, more numb the longer the bullying went on.

"You're useless, you should kill yourself," spat one of the main instigators during lunch period one cold November day. She shoved me to the floor of an empty classroom. As she kicked me in the side for good measure, I thought perhaps she was right. Maybe killing myself wasn't a bad idea. I wished she'd kicked me harder. I just wanted to feel... something.

"Oops!" one of her minions giggled one night at a party, pouring her soft drink over me. Smacking me repeatedly in the head with the now-empty bottle, she smiled as other kids looked on, unmoved. At home afterwards, I went straight to my room, nursing a headache and a heavy heart.

No More Fairy Tales

In January of my thirteenth year, my parents separated for good. My father had been working away more and more frequently. As he prepared to leave on yet another business trip after spending one final weekend at home, he told my brother and me he wouldn't be coming back. As he closed the door, he left behind a blast of frigid winter air; I felt the last vestiges of childhood slip out with him. I watched him drive away as my tears ran unchecked. It was time to stop believing in fairy tales.

Monday, after school, my best friend Chelsea and I went to the movies to see a new release: *A Walk to Remember*. In the movie, Landon Carter is a teenager being raised by a single mother. In one dramatic scene, an encounter with his estranged father leaves Landon disappointed once again. As Landon angrily storms off, his father implores him not to walk away, to which Landon responds, "You taught me how." I could not stop crying for the rest of the movie.

The divorce proceedings that followed my father's departure were less than amicable. There were lawyers, court dates and awful things said. I began keeping secrets. I learned to manipulate my other family members to find out what both my parents were up to, information that wasn't shared with me directly. I became adept at playing a game I thought of as emotional chess. I viewed interactions between certain family members as turns in a game; I would try to predict their next move so I could make mine first. By staying several steps ahead, I found it easier to feign indifference when eventually confronted with the next painful truth. Whose side was I supposed to be on that day? Who were my parents dating, since when, and what did those new relationships mean for me? I began to see people as wholly unreliable. The only thing I knew for certain was that people lie and people leave.

Since Dad had partial custody of my brother and me, he bought a house near the family home where my mom still lived. Things were not easy between us; my dad and I fought constantly. I couldn't forgive him for leaving, or for moving on, and he didn't know how to handle my anger. At fourteen, I made the torturous decision to no longer live with him, or even see him. I figured it was best for both of us. On a bleak November afternoon, I gathered up a few of my most cherished possessions—a couple of my favourite CDs, some makeup, and signed photos of boy bands I loved—and stuffed them into my purse. I left the suburbs and headed for the city to see my friends, drawing comfort from the false familiarity of our frequent haunts. Resolute, I shed no tears that day.

Not living with my dad meant losing contact with a large part of my extended family. The people I'd seen practically every week since my birth were no longer part of my life.

Interrupted Plans

I was fourteen years old the first time I made concrete plans to die. The previous year, shortly after Christmas, we received a phone call about a beloved family friend who had died that day by suicide. When my mom put down the phone and ran out of the room sobbing her name, I knew she was gone. She had been so alive the day before. What had happened in just one day? When had she known she was going to take her life? She had been a good and giving person, dearly loved by so many. Had she not felt that? I'd never really thought about suicide before, but while I asked myself these questions, it suddenly seemed like a perfectly reasonable and natural solution. While others wondered how she could possibly do it, I understood. Who wouldn't want to plan their own exit if life got to be too much? In a way, I admired her decision.

My suicide plan wasn't long in the making, perhaps only a few weeks. Every Thursday evening, my mom and brother had night classes, so I was alone in the house. After my dad left, there was a car in the garage that nobody drove. I decided to die by carbon monoxide poisoning on one such Thursday night. The night before, I wrote a letter, briefly addressing some of the most important people in my life. I told them I was sorry. I wrote it in braille; only a few people would be able to read it. It was January in Northern Canada, so I planned to get cozy with my pillow and blankets, fall asleep and never wake up again. I now know that death by carbon monoxide poisoning is often not nearly that tranquil.

On that fateful Thursday, the car my mom usually drove needed servicing, and by Thursday evening, the garage was empty. My death would have to wait.

The next week at school, I was summoned to the guidance counsellor's office. A tiny spitfire of a woman in her early forties with an infectious laugh, she was oddly subdued as she invited me into her small, windowless office and asked me to take a seat. She told me someone was concerned about me. She didn't say who or why. Perhaps it was because of a poem I had written—about the funeral of a teenage girl who had died by suicide— and published semi-anonymously online. "Do you have a plan?" the counsellor calmly asked.

"Not really," I lied. "Maybe some pills or something."

She called my house that afternoon, and that week, my mom took me to see a psychologist. I sat stiffly in a plush armchair in his dimly lit wood-panelled office, my feet resting on what felt like a thick, expensive oriental rug, breathing in the smell of musty old books and furniture polish. Doctor Faulkner talked to me like I was a textbook case, assuming I was depressed because I blamed myself for my parents' divorce. I listened to the clock on his desk tick loudly, counting down the seconds until I could leave. I figured maybe he was better with adults. Although the several sessions with him weren't overly helpful, the interruption was enough for me to put my plan on hold... for the time being. Next time I'd get it right.

In addition to my regular meetings with the school's guidance counsellor, I was referred to a social worker to help me sort through some of the problems I was having at home. She was phenomenal, showing just the right amount of compassion while actively helping me deal with complex feelings and emotions in various areas of my life. When she was transferred, I chose not to attend sessions with a different social worker, believing I was unlikely to find another like her.

I Can't Fix This

During this already confusing time, I was affected by sexual violence. The perpetrator was a "trusted" adult who I'd known for years. I leaned on him for support throughout my parents' divorce, the bullying at school, and my subsequent depression. He knew my darkest secrets and deepest fears. This meant that he also knew what to say to keep me quiet. It was the worst kind of betrayal.

Thoughts of his betrayal came to me at the most inopportune moments: the pungent smell of cheap cologne and greasy hair; my muscles growing taut beneath unwelcome hands; the bitter taste of fear and shame on my tongue; the way those feelings twisted in my gut; and the weak protestations that died on my lips. I heard the belittling insults about my body and appearance, and the calm assurances that I was powerless to stop this. I had nightmares and intense feelings of sadness, guilt and anger, mostly toward myself. I told myself it was my fault, that maybe it was what I secretly wanted, that I didn't have the right to feel this way because it could have been so much worse.

Years later, shortly before I graduated from high school, someone who was completely unaware of my history mentioned that another young girl had been preyed upon by the same man. I had to run to the bathroom to be sick. He had expertly exploited her weaknesses, as he had done with mine. This was the cost of my selfish silence. I knew I did not and could not make his decisions for him, but could I have stopped it? I hated myself; her pain was a cross I would forever bear.

Although the girl was no more than an acquaintance, with whom I'd never discussed our shared experience, I wrote her a song with the hope she would hear it and understand. I followed her social media for years; I needed to know she was okay, that she had made a good life for herself.

Meanwhile, in my first year of high school, my brother told me my father's cancer was back, after having been in remission for ten years. I went to see him in the hospital after he'd had a long and complex surgery to remove as much of the cancer as possible. I couldn't believe how frail he had become since I'd last seen him. The same year, he suffered a heart attack. Although he eventually recovered from his illnesses, at the time, in the self-absorbed way of a teenager, I couldn't help but begin to wonder if I'd somehow played a part in it all.

The confusion and guilt of all these things together was too much. I experimented with self-harm, seeking comfort from the blade of the folding knife I kept in the jewelry box on my dresser. I didn't experience any of the relief I'd heard could come from the physical pain. In a desperate attempt to find solace, I also tried purging a few times, but that offered no peace.

As my self-awareness grew over my teen years, I realized that no matter how many people I educated about blindness, there would always be more. There would forever be battles over access to information and opportunities to fight. My capabilities would frequently be called into question. I would always know discrimination. By fifteen years old, I'd already grown world weary.

While there were many days when I could laugh at my situation, regaling my friends and family with ridiculous stories of the things people said and did because of my blindness, there were other days when it felt like a nightmare I could never wake up from. All I could think on those dark days was: *This is forever. It will never change. I can't fix this.*

A Safe Place

In my awkward teenage years, I began to take refuge in music, despite my previous disinterest in lessons. In high school, I took as many music classes in and out of school as I could. I spent many boring history periods feverishly writing song lyrics while the teacher droned on. Eventually, I returned to piano lessons in order to learn to accompany myself while singing. I was frequently chosen to represent my school's music program at outreach events, and relished my time spent in the band room. I'd finally found a safe place. As soon as I walked through that classroom door, I was untouchable. There, I got respect.

As I delved further into music, things came together quickly. At fifteen years old, I placed in the finals of a regional talent competition, performing a ballad I had written about the loneliness and isolation of my teen years. It was a surreal experience. Even though I was one of the youngest contestants, I made it through the preliminaries to the semifinals, and then onto the finals. On that last night, after the winner was announced and the curtains closed, I was approached backstage by Brock, a producer who had been on the panel of judges. He explained who he was and what he did, then handed me his card and told me to give him a call. I was shocked and humbled that an industry professional had even taken the time to show interest in my music, but I didn't let myself believe anything would come of it. I had barely performed outside of school events, let alone a recording studio.

With trepidation, I reached out to Brock right away, even as I told myself I would never hear back from him. I was wrong. Later that same week, over chai lattes in an artsy downtown coffee shop, we made plans to record an album in the coming months. That night backstage, I had met someone who would alter the path of my life, a man who would throw me a lifeline to cling to in those dark years.

During the weeks that followed, Brock and I spent hours shaping my songs and preparing them for the studio. With his gentle guidance, I learned everything from technique and music theory to arranging songs for a band, and the ins and outs of recording. When the day finally came, and I walked into the studio for the first time, I was as ready as I could possibly be.

For as long as I live, I will never forget the feeling of putting those studio headphones on and stepping into the recording booth for the first time. It felt like I'd finally found my place in this world. The recording studio is a perfectionist's haven. How many other opportunities do we get in life to erase our mistakes? I drank it all in, the skill and kindness of the session musicians, the studio lingo, the smell of dusty instruments and old cigarette smoke.

A quiet hero, Brock gave of himself so completely, a constant support and encouraging voice as I took my first steps into the world of professional music. He was there through fourteen-hour studio days and at every show, either playing alongside me or content to cheer me on from the audience. In the studio, if I became frustrated by a vocal line I just couldn't get right, I would hear his voice in my headphones, making up hilarious parodies of my songs. I would laugh, my frustration forgotten. I usually nailed the difficult line on the next try. If one of my performances didn't go well, he managed to console me and give me constructive feedback at the same time.

Months after that first day in the studio, on a warm spring night, I stepped out onstage at my first CD release concert. I looked like a gothic fairy in a dress with a tight velvet bodice and layers of artfully torn black lace, which billowed about me, ending just above my bare feet. My waist-length hair, dyed jet black at the time, cascaded in waves down my back. The club was packed with people I knew, and many I didn't. I held Brock's arm as we walked to the grand piano, accompanied by raucous cheers. My heart pounded and my hands tingled with nervous anticipation. The stage lights warm on my bare arms and face—I was aglow. The rest of the band had already taken their places, and we energetically launched into the first song. The most incredible feeling came over me. I knew I had been born to live this moment.

"Wow, there are so many of you," I said when the cheers had died down after the first song, laughing a little. I felt dazed. "Thank you so much for being here." Each one of these people had come to see me play, to celebrate the release of my first album. I struggled to take in the magnitude of it all.

When the final chords of the last song had faded away into wild applause as the audience rose to its feet, I practically floated backstage. After a massive group hug and quick celebration with the musicians, I headed to the front of the venue, planning to chat with people from behind the merch table where my CD was being sold. I never made it there. As soon as I emerged, I was surrounded. Every way I turned, there were people offering congratulatory hugs and handshakes, thrusting flowers into my hands, and holding out CDs for me to sign. I could not have been more grateful, or felt more loved, than I did on that night.

The memories I hold of music during my teen years are my favourites, a source of pride. Those experiences were a healthy outlet for processing huge, complicated teenage emotions. I was treated as an equal, even by seasoned professional musicians; they helped me feel capable and valued. To them, I was just a girl who loved music.

Caught Between Two Worlds

In stark contrast to my primary school years, filled with teachers who encouraged my academic success and fostered my creativity, my high school education provided little of what I needed. The year before I entered my new high school, we had several meetings with school officials. The overarching theme was that there was no money to support *my* education. I felt like an unwanted nuisance.

School officials discouraged me from taking advanced classes, not because I didn't have the marks to get into them, but because they feared there would be too much work for me. Translation: More material would need to be transcribed into braille, taking up more time and money in an already overstretched public school system. Their reluctance to allow me to take these courses only made me more determined to do just that.

Some of my male classmates weren't much better than the hostile girls. They'd steal my cane to see how I could manage without it. A group of boys took to silently grabbing me and holding me against them in a bear hug. As someone who was dealing with recent trauma, and could barely stand to be touched, these games were extremely distressing. Asking them to stop only made them do it more. If I mentioned it to anyone in authority, they'd say that the boys liked me and just didn't know how to show it. Boys will be boys and all that.

One day in the eleventh grade, I'd finally had enough of the games. My heart pounding, I tried to recoil from the boy who had grabbed me. With his thick, ropey arms wrapped tightly around me, he wouldn't let go, despite my repeated requests for him to do so. Something inside of me snapped. Pushing against him with my full weight, I shoved him backward, breaking his hold. Using the element of surprise and sudden momentum, I brought the metal end of my cane up to connect none too gently with his crotch. Standing over him as he rolled around on the hallway floor, clutching himself in agony, I felt a grim sense of satisfaction. "I fucking warned you fifty times," I said coldly as I turned away in disgust and melted into the noisy throng of students heading to class. The bullies never touched me again.

At seventeen, I found myself in a psychologist's office once more. After learning of the other girl who had suffered at the hands of the man who had hurt me, the guilt of feeling I should have done more to protect her had become too much to overcome alone. Although years had passed since I'd last seen him, memories of my own experience once again troubled me, creeping into my dreams, and making it difficult to concentrate in class.

Doctor Anna, as her patients called her, had come highly recommended. She was raven-haired and beautiful, with a penchant for wearing colourful shirts—so bright even I could see them—and a ton of silver bangles that jangled together on her wrists every time she moved. I left most of our sessions feeling frustrated.

"Now, imagine that you're back there, imagine yourself screaming and someone hearing you," she'd say. "Imagine fighting, imagine someone was there and stepped in to defend you. Imagine that you had told someone right away, the first time it happened."

I would become more and more anxious throughout the sessions, the office closing in on me. Even though her office was cheerily decorated, the heat was suffocating and the odour of Chinese food from the restaurant downstairs nauseated me. I now know she was trying to empower me to change the narrative of my experience, but at the time it felt like rubbing salt in a wound. She pointed out everything I should have done but didn't do. I didn't see the point in telling myself a different story because, in the end, it would be only that: a made-up story. In the real world, I had still failed.

As my friends gained more independence with age, I began to feel frustrated and alone. Although I was able to take public transportation and navigate malls and stores by myself, my friends started driving. The world opened up to them in a way it never would for me. I struggled with spontaneity. When my friends would jump in the car and meet up wherever they pleased, I needed to adhere to bus schedules, and practice the route several times beforehand, or beg a ride from someone.

31

Getting turned around while out in public became my biggest fear. I couldn't let strangers see me fail, because it would only confirm what I felt so many of them already believed about my capabilities, or lack thereof. If I did get lost and needed to backtrack, or God forbid, call someone to get me out of my mess, I would beat myself up about it for days, sometimes weeks or even months. I couldn't let it go. When I was outside the safety of my four walls, I needed to be 100 percent perfect all the time.

When friends got summer jobs, I worried about finding an entry level job that didn't require the use of a cash register. I agonized over whether to disclose my blindness ahead of time and risk not getting an interview. If I waited until the interview, I had to hope the potential employer didn't waste time on irrelevant personal questions, rather than asking what skills I could bring to the company.

As I grew more interested in makeup and fashion, I realized that my choices were filtered through someone else's perception of what I might want. If someone said a particular colour of eyeshadow looked good on me, or a shirt wasn't the right colour for my complexion, I wondered what it would be like to know these things for myself. What if I actually really liked that colour? It was just their preference after all. As my friends and I would get ready for a night out, I'd wonder how it would be to glance in the mirror on the way out the door and think to myself that, despite my imperfections, that night I was beautiful.

I often felt caught between two worlds. Blind people who hung out with other blind people seemed to almost have their own culture, which even went as far as to have its own slang. I never felt completely part of that group. Many of the blind people I met were extremely sheltered, and I got the impression that some of their parents didn't like me much. Although I was by no means a wild child, my involvement in the typical, mildly nefarious things teenagers do was often construed as a negative influence on the children whom those parents fought so hard to protect. My exceptionally long, black hair and my black attire, complete with fishnets, chains and dark eye makeup, likely didn't help matters. I was too influenced by the greater world's cliques to be fully accepted into the insular world of the blind. Yet, that greater society was intent on reminding me I didn't belong there either.

My early romantic relationships never ended well. Boyfriends complained that I was too detached, and they had no idea how I felt about them. I could be intentionally cruel and prided myself on being aloof. I suppose I wanted to cause another the pain of abandonment. While I enjoyed the chase and the initial excitement of new romance, all the sweet words of young love and the hands on my body sickened me. I would quickly end things if I felt they were getting too serious, or if I sensed the boy would soon move on. Never again would I give anyone an opportunity to leave. I was called an ice queen, a bitch and a tease, but I didn't care. I was taking back control.

High school classes weren't smooth sailing by any means. I would commonly go without textbooks, class notes and assignments, and I didn't have an accessible calculator for math until shortly before I wrote my final grade 12 math exam. I was expected to either dictate the equations to someone else who would input them into a calculator, or do the math in my head.

"I don't know what they want me to do," I overheard my math teacher saying to a colleague one day. "She's just not good at math. Some kids aren't." She shrugged helplessly.

I bit back a retort. *A calculator and some class notes might be a start.*

In the twelfth grade, I finally got a taste of a quality high school education. To our knowledge, I was the first blind person to take high school courses online. I was enrolled part-time in a cyber school. The support staff were excited by my enrolment and welcomed me enthusiastically. We were all on the same team, determined to make this work. The staff provided me with the technical support I needed to ensure that their program was compatible with my screen reader— software that works by converting everything on the screen into synthesized speech or braille.

For the first time in my high school education, I received all of my coursework at the same moment as my classmates. At cyber school, nobody complained about how much work it was to have me in their program, or about the money my educational supports cost them.

Having never met me in person, my classmates were unaware of my blindness. It was exhilarating to be just another student in the class. The flexibility afforded by being able to study on my own time also allowed me the freedom to pursue my increasing involvement in extra-curricular activities, namely music. I began to enjoy learning again, in a way I hadn't for years.

While I would have loved to attend cyber school full-time, I was obligated to take some classes in person at my regular high school. This would apparently allow for social interaction I neither wanted nor benefited from. I learned that it was relatively easy for me to cut class; adults tended to take what I told them at face value. For some strange reason, they seemed to believe that people with disabilities always tell the truth. Apart from music classes taught by my favourite high school teacher, life at school was soul crushing; all I could think about was graduating and getting the hell out.

One fall day, I was called to the classroom of one of the English teachers. I had never been in any of her classes. "I've got a copy of the CD you released last year," she told me. "Would you be interested in writing a song and performing it at your graduation?"

"Sure," I said without hesitation. I saw a perfect opportunity. My entire graduating class was going to hear exactly what I wanted to tell them.

The song I wrote, while inspiring and uplifting on the surface, contained a few carefully veiled insults directed at some of the people who had tormented me for years.

I sat at the grand piano that day in May, in a dress that clung to my body because of the oppressive heat. My palms slick with sweat, I let my gaze roam over the rows of faces I couldn't see. Many of these people had never really seen me either. There was not a sound from the audience. For what felt like the first time, all my classmates were listening to what I had to say.

After the ceremony, a boy who had been in many of my classes throughout high school approached me. "Wow," he said, "I didn't even know you could talk, let alone sing."

I shrugged. "I guess you never listened."

Graduating and moving on to university, where I planned to major in psychology, felt like a great weight had finally been lifted from my chest. I had so much hope for the future, so much faith that I would soon come into my own.

The Sports Car

As high school drew to a close and I prepared to branch out in the world, I began thinking a guide dog might make navigating my busy life a little easier. Choosing a guide dog school is a bit like choosing a college. Each program offers something a little different, and there are pros and cons to each option. Did I want to travel to the guide dog school and live in a dorm during the training period, or would I rather have a trainer work with me at home? Could I fully commit to an intensive training program—typically lasting two to four weeks? What was the client-to-instructor ratio in class? What methods did the school employ to train their dogs? Did I want a trainer to follow up with me in person at set intervals, or did I want support only if and when I ran into a problem? Upon graduating, did I want to own the dog immediately, or was it okay if the school retained ownership? Was there any support offered to cover veterinary expenses? The list of questions was long and overwhelming, but by grade 12, I had made my selection.

After an in-depth application process involving numerous questionnaires, personal references and notes from my doctors, a guide dog mobility instructor came to my home to evaluate how I travelled independently. Could I navigate confidently using my cane without getting lost? Was I aware of my surroundings? Could I tell by the traffic noise when it was safe to cross at a lighted intersection? Was I strong enough physically to handle a large dog? Knowing which dogs were currently in training, was there one that would be a good fit for my walking pace, personality and lifestyle? I needed a dog who was driven enough to handle busy environments and long days, but content to lie quietly during university lectures, who would be happy living with cats and other dogs, and who would be comfortable on the stage during my performances.

The trainer brought Simba, a guide dog in training, with her to the interview. While she walked behind holding the leash, I picked up the harness and gave the command "forward" and we were off, flying down the street faster than I'd ever walked with my cane. I felt light, unencumbered. As the trainer was leaving, she told me I would know within a few weeks if I would be accepted to receive a dog from that particular school.

The anxious wait began. True to her word, three weeks later, I got the call. I would train with my first guide dog that summer, before I headed off to university. On a sweltering day in early August, a trainer arrived at my home with a two-year-old black Labrador golden retriever cross. My new partner, Bibby, was jokingly called "The Sports Car" by her trainers because she was small, fast and sleek.

After a quiet weekend spent getting to know one another, Bibby and I began a rigorous three-week training period with a guide dog mobility instructor. For eight hours a day, we trained together in all kinds of environments, from crowded shopping malls to subway stations to country roads, and in all kinds of weather— walking in the scalding sun and the pouring rain. After the hands-on portion of the day, I had lectures on dog care, training and behaviour.

Contrary to the stories in guide dog school brochures, many guide dog partnerships don't have a fairytale beginning, with dog and handler gliding effortlessly off into the sunset. After a rocky first year of bruises, caused by her lack of attention or my failure to read her signals, Bibby and I finally meshed, forming an incredible team. We moved as one down busy downtown streets, a *pas de deux* in perfect sync. Eventually, we knew what the other would do, moments before we acted. Words were wholly unnecessary. What Bibby lacked in size, she more than made up for in personality. She unfailingly loved everyone she met, human and animal alike, but was headstrong and had her own definite ideas about how things should happen.

A common misconception is that guide dogs know where to go on their own. While they will often learn the routes their handler takes frequently, they do not have some GPS implant that allows them to lead their handler across the city to a destination they've never been before. They require specific instructions in unfamiliar environments; the handler directs the dog using commands such as right, left, back and forward. The impressive thing about guide dogs is their "intelligent disobedience." A dog will wilfully disobey a directive given by the handler if it thinks it is unsafe to proceed—such as reaching the edge of a drop-off like a subway platform, or coming upon an obstacle that has no clear path around it. They also do not indicate when it's safe to cross the street, although they will practice intelligent disobedience if they notice a car they think the handler does not. The dog's job is to guide their handler safely around obstacles, and the handler's job is to direct them to their destination. While a guide dog's training and temperament is admirable, it isn't magic.

Canes are obstacle finders while guide dogs are obstacle avoiders. Unfortunately, while Bibby's presence afforded me increased mobility, it also attracted "obstacles" I would have preferred to avoid. While a more sociable person might enjoy the conversation invited by having a dog in places where dogs don't normally go, I dreaded it, and experienced increased anxiety while out in public. Studying for an upcoming exam in the library or going out to dinner with friends, I couldn't stand it when strangers interrupted us, rapidly firing questions as if their very lives depended on knowing the name, age and breed of my dog. Then, after exclaiming "Oh, she must be your best friend! She takes such good care of you!" in a voice normally reserved for two-year-olds, they would pat me on the head and go on their merry way. If I was by myself or caught off guard by a question, I often felt obligated to answer truthfully. I struggled with setting firm boundaries.

Sometimes however, while out with friends, I would have fun with the intruders, making up ridiculous answers. as I waited outside a theatre before a show, an old woman passing by stopped abruptly next to me. "What a special friend you have! Your sweet doggy must help you out so much!" she exclaimed in a sugary voice that set my teeth on edge.

"Absolutely!" I answered with equal enthusiasm. "Actually, next week, I'm having my car fitted with special controls so she can drive me everywhere. It'll be a huge help!".

The woman hesitated. "Oh… that's nice dear," she said as she turned and walked away, a cloud of old lady perfume lingering behind her. My friends roared with laughter.

When someone asked a question about my dog or my blindness that I found invasive, occasionally I would act utterly confused. "Sorry, no English," I would say in an exaggerated Hispanic accent. This tactic was especially amusing if I was chatting with a friend, with whom I would then continue my conversation loudly, in perfect English. If someone asked me, "Are you really blind?" I'd shrug. "Nah, it's fun to pretend though. And I get to ride the bus for free."

When a random person would plunk themselves down next to me on the bus and, without even introducing themselves first, ask if I was born "that way"

I'd ask them what they were talking about rather than tell them that my medical history was none of their damn business. This effectively put the discomfort back on them. Other times, I would respond with, "Were you?" When they asked what I meant, I would say, *"You know, were you born… like that?"* They usually got flustered and dropped their line of questioning. To this day, I still get the urge to respond, "Were you born stupid?" but I have thus far managed to keep my inside voice from turning into my outside voice... for the most part.

All this unwanted attention wore on me. I began to dread going out, afraid Bibby or I would make a mistake and invite a myriad of comments from the peanut gallery who had clearly watched way too many episodes of *The Dog Whisperer*. I especially disliked comments like "Oh, the dog must still be in training" from uneducated windbags who believed guide dogs are like the infallible robot dogs they saw on Animal Planet and not the highly trained dogs they are, who sometimes forget their training and do typical dog things.

I was irritated by constant comments like *"You're so lucky, I wish I could have a dog I could take everywhere!"* While I would smile and nod, inside I'd be thinking, *Stare at the sun long enough and you can.* I would gladly give up my perceived special privileges for equality, to not be pleasantly surprised by a completely mundane interaction or conversation with a stranger, because these mundane conversations would be the norm instead of the exception.

"Look Tommy! That nice doggy is that lady's eyes!" was a refrain that followed me everywhere I went. I'd never asked to be little Tommy's teachable moment. I just wanted to blend in.

Unlike a cane, a dog is not something you can fold up and tuck away when you don't want to be noticed in public. Even on the bus, Bibby was visible enough under the seat that I was afforded little peace. One morning, a woman stood at the front of the bus and loudly proclaimed, "Wow! I thought *my* life was bad, but then I saw *her.* If I went blind, I'd honestly have to kill myself." She hurried down the steps out of the bus, leaving a stunned silence in her wake. Any witty retorts I could have used only came to me long after the bus doors had closed. Feeling the burn of so many pairs of eyes on me, I got off at the next stop and walked the rest of the way.

That woman publicly announced an opinion that wasn't an uncommon sentiment. "I don't know how you do it, I'd kill myself," strangers would say "sympathetically." How could I make them understand that blindness wasn't the issue; the problem was their perception of it. They would project their fears onto me, assuming I must feel the same as they would should they lose their sight. In their narrow view of blindness, they didn't understand that I'd had a lifetime of practice at being blind.

I led a full existence. Ironically, the people making these insensitive and simplistic comments never realized *they* were the problem.

My friends and family also received increased attention while out in public with me. They sometimes got the same kind of praise as Bibby. People approached us out of nowhere to tell them how kind they were for "taking care of me." If I was walking arm-in-arm with a female friend, passersby would remark that we must be lesbians. I was used to the unwelcome attention, but it infuriated me when my loved ones had to endure it as well. It was completely unfair to them. Sometimes I wondered if they would rather not be seen in public with me.

Annoyances about increased public visibility aside, not everyone loved Bibby. Although the law supposedly protected my right to have her accompany me into places where dogs are not normally permitted, we were often asked to leave stores and restaurants. People would occasionally scream in abject terror when they saw us heading their way.

One evening, a few weeks after moving to a new city, I boarded a bus driven by a man who was very obviously uncomfortable having a dog on his bus—so much so that he failed to stop where I had requested him to. Angered, he kept driving the now-empty bus to a different stop where, he claimed, another bus would arrive to take me back. This "bus stop" was on the other side of a highway, bordered by farmland and a steep ditch. I waited and waited, and not even a car drove by. The sun had set completely, and there were no streetlights along this stretch of highway. I shivered. It started to rain, and still no bus came. I didn't know where I was. These were the days before a person's current location could be shared with just a few taps on a smartphone. Hours later, a passerby found me in tears: both Bibby and I were soaked and chilled to the bone.

The bus company was suspiciously unable to track down the driver. His union afforded him the protection he had not given me.

Bibby was a sensitive, anxious dog; she fed off my anxiety. The stress of public access work became too much for her. She began showing fear of crowded spaces, refusing to enter buses or busy shopping malls. Feeling ill-equipped to handle the extra scrutiny that came with guide dog ownership, I retired Bibby and kept her as a loved pet. I did not apply for a successor dog.

Misadventures in Blindness

Being a young girl travelling alone in big cities, I quickly learned there were definite disadvantages to a cane instead of a dog. First off, using a cane seemed to invite more stealth grabbers, people who would sneak up behind me and, without a word, propel me in the direction they assumed I wanted to go. Worse than an innocent stealth grabber were creepy men who would "accidentally" cop a feel under the guise of offering assistance I had neither asked for nor wanted. It happened often enough that I could predict who they would be with stunning accuracy and, eventually, I came to view it with a weary acceptance instead of the violation it clearly was.

Many times, stealth grabbers would not let go of me, even after I asked them to. I realized that, in the eyes of many, my body was not my own. I would be looked down upon if I rebuffed these violations of my bodily autonomy, because, after all, they were just "trying to help" and what kind of bitter, ungrateful bitch wouldn't accept help? Oh darn, now I've gone and ruined it for the next blind person, because that "helpful person" won't ever be so kind to another blind person again.

I put a lot of pressure on myself to be what I thought was a good ambassador for people in my minority. If a strange man came up behind an able-bodied female, grabbing her without a word and pushing her in a different direction, the expected and encouraged response would be for the female to defend herself. I soon learned, however, in my case, it was easier to shut up and take it and to put the comfort and dignity of complete strangers ahead of my own. How dare I offend or embarrass a good person who was only trying to lend me a helping hand?

One afternoon, as I used my cane to navigate the empty-feeling downtown sidewalks on my way to the subway, a disheveled man accosted me, determined to help. I repeatedly declined. Even outdoors, the waves of alcohol and body odour coming off of him were overpowering. He walked with me for several blocks, ignoring my increasingly uncomfortable pleas to leave me alone. He followed me down into the crowded subway station and I waited for several trains to pass, hoping he would get on one of them. Finally, when I hadn't heard him speak for a long time, I figured he was gone. I boarded my train home, only to be approached by two police officers.

"Would you mind stepping off the train at the next stop?" one of the officers asked me quietly. I was perplexed.

"Do you know the man who walked into the station with you?" asked the other officer, the older of the pair, once we were standing on the platform at the next station.

"No…" I said, growing more confused.

"We didn't think so. He's someone who is known to us, and we watched him enter the station with you and then follow you onto the train," the first officer explained. "We asked you to get off the train to make sure he didn't continue to follow you. We would have dealt with him if he had also gotten off at this stop. This is the kind of thing he does."

The officers waited with me on the platform for a few more trains to pass, then sent me on my way. The walk home was tense.

People I told this story to loved to tell me all the things I'd done wrong. I should have called 911. I should have picked up the security phone at the station. I should have yelled for help. My instincts, honed after years of unsolicited "help" from people of all walks of life, told me not to rock the boat, that it was better to keep moving than to stop and pull out my phone to make a call. Knowing the location of my pursuer at all times, while navigating heavy downtown traffic, took all my concentration. Every one of the critics was able-bodied and would likely never find themselves in such a situation. These people would never fully understand that however unfair it is, the rules of respect don't apply equally across the board.

One morning as I waited, with just my cane, to cross a busy downtown intersection, I sensed two young men waiting with me. "You can cross now," said one of them, just as a bus drove through the intersection. Luckily, I had strong enough orientation skills, and little enough faith in humanity, to ignore him. I wanted to chalk it up to an innocent mistake, and I would have, had the boys not run off, laughing hysterically.

I missed Bibby on those long walks home after dark, especially when random men offered to walk with me. I never told them where I lived but, as hard as I listened, I could never be completely sure they weren't following me at a distance. I missed the safety of my furry companion's presence when I endured the whistles and cat calls women are loath to put up with, however mine often came with a twist.

On a spring evening, I was walking to a pub to meet up with some friends. I felt fantastic, brimming with confidence and looking forward to a fun night out. It was the first day I'd been able to put away my heavy winter sweaters, a day when the world begins to emerge from its winter slumber and promises warm summer days ahead. As I walked, lost in thoughts of the evening's upcoming festivities, a man called down to me from an apartment balcony. "Hey! Hey you! What's your number?"

His friend, standing beside him at the railing, shushed him. "Dude!" he admonished. "She's blind! Blind people don't have phones."

A common pickup line I heard was "Blind chicks are the best, you wouldn't even know if I was like, really ugly or something."

"Oh, believe me, I know," I'd say sardonically.

"You must not really be blind then," they'd shoot back, their male pride injured.

What they didn't realize was how much "visual" information I could pick up in other ways. It isn't that my other senses are better than those of a sighted person, I have just learned to use them more effectively, to pay attention to small nuances that a sighted person may miss. The sound of a person's voice gives me a good estimate of their age; their gait or a simple handshake can tell me their approximate size and stature. Paying attention to what is, or is not, said about a person, as well as how others react to them, can give me clues as to their physical appearance. The sound and smell of a room, or the feel of the sun on my face, or the wind in my hair allows me to make visual sense of the environment. I still interpret and speak about visual imagery as a sighted person might, I just process it differently to reach the same conclusions. This is why you will never hear a blind person say they "listened" to a movie. We watch movies and listen to music. End of story. And no, we really, really don't want to feel your face, thanks though.

Some of my friends enjoyed helping me mess with peoples' heads. A guy I vaguely recognized as being in one of my university classes once asked me, "When you wake up each morning, are you scared because overnight you forgot you were blind?" I somehow managed to keep a straight face.

"Yeah, it's terrifying. I don't want to talk about it, please don't remind me." I let my voice crack with false emotion. Perhaps I wouldn't have won an Oscar, but it was a pretty solid performance.

A friend sitting next to me at the time chimed in. "Seriously? That is actually the most idiotic question I have ever heard!" We burst out laughing. I don't think the guy who had asked the question thought it was funny.

Sometimes, I admit, my friends and I took things too far when reacting to a perceived slight. While waiting in line at a mall kiosk on a busy Saturday afternoon, a woman surreptitiously cut in front of me, figuring I wouldn't notice. A sighted friend was standing behind me; the lady obviously didn't realize we were together. My friend whispered to me, telling me what she had done. Being young and stupid, I decided I'd make her think twice before doing it again. Just as she turned to leave, with perfect timing, I stuck my cane out to the side, just the tiniest bit. I had only intended for her to stumble, but... time seemed to slow as she teetered, then fell in epic fashion. Bags and boxes scattered around her with a mighty crash. Leaping to her feet, she apologized to *me* profusely, then scrambled to pick up all her strewn items. I felt like a terrible person but, at the same time, tried unsuccessfully to suppress my laughter.

We could also mess with people completely by accident. Coming out of a bar one night, a friend asked to try my cane. Most of my friends have done this at some point or another, so I handed it to him. I knew this part of town well, so I walked beside him, ensuring he didn't walk out into traffic and get himself killed as he closed his eyes. He stumbled along, both from the effects of alcohol and his sudden loss of vision, and a group of partiers approached us. "Oh my God!" screeched one of the girls. "You guys stole that from some poor blind person! That's sick."

Her male friend, overflowing with testosterone and booze, added, "You guys wanna fight? That's messed up, stealing from a blind person!"

"Let's go! Hurry!" someone in our group yelled. I grabbed my cane back from my friend and we all sprinted toward the subway station. Cries of "You're all going to hell!" receded behind us. In the safety of the station, we doubled over, laughing until our sides hurt and tears ran down our faces.

Friends, Fun, Love, and Antidepressants

My first few years of university were everything I hoped school would be. I could finally focus on my studies, instead of spending time advocating for the educational support I had lacked in high school. As with my brief time in cyber school, I had textbooks, handouts and exams at the same time as my classmates, and I quickly made friends in my classes.

Things weren't perfect though. While most students had matured, some little assholes simply grew into big assholes. During one memorable rhetoric class, I listened to students sincerely stating their opinions that obese and disabled people should be segregated onto our own planes. The professor laughed. My face burned with shame; I quietly gathered my things and slipped out the door before the lecture ended. The next day, I went to the registrar's office and dropped the course. I then picked up an English class taught by a professor who happened to be blind. I would listen to students make fun of his blindness before class; they didn't seem to notice or care that their insults equally applied to me, and that I could hear every cruel word.

My major, psychology, wasn't quite what I'd hoped for. It seemed to be based more in science than compassion. In my immaturity, I couldn't see the big picture. To effectively help someone, both compassion and sound, scientific knowledge are needed.

During the summer break after my first year of university, I received a government arts grant to record my second album. Thrilled, I began to organize producers, audio engineers and session players. It was during this project that I met Jordan, a session bass player I hired to play on the album, and now my partner.

When he arrived at my house for a band rehearsal on the day we met, I wordlessly handed him the sheet music for my songs. Painfully shy, I had no idea what to say. All through rehearsal, we never spoke to each other directly.

"So, seven-thirty on Thursday for the next practice?" he asked me at the end of rehearsal, zipping his bass back into its case.

"Yeah…" I answered stupidly.

In the music world, people often say many relationships start (and end) in recording studios. The camaraderie was strong between the musicians working on the project, and some of us began to spend time together outside the studio, working on other recordings or just hanging out. The studio was in a rougher part of town, and each day when we had finished, Jordan would drive me home. Thankfully by that point, I was able to speak more than one word to him. We would chat animatedly the whole 45-minute drive to my house. It wasn't until we'd finished the project that I learned Jordan lived in the other direction.

Our first date wasn't really a date at all. As an excuse to spend time together, we met up to record the piano track for another project I'd been asked to collaborate on. We worked late into the night. I knew I was smitten when he let me drive his car that night. Not everyone is so brave, or so crazy, as to get into a vehicle with me behind the wheel.

It was a sweet summer romance. During those all-too-short weeks, we often stayed out all night, rolling in as the sun rose over the prairies, just in time to head off to work. We wanted to spend as much time together as we could, because we knew it would soon come to an end. Come fall, Jordan would be starting university 1200 kilometres away.

Once he'd moved, we survived a year that included many white-knuckled drives on wintery mountain passes for him, and frequent flights for me. As the school year wore on, I became more and more disenchanted with my choice of major and the city I called home. I was tired of the cold and snow, the darkness that arrived at 4:00 PM in the winter. I was unsure of what I really wanted to do with my education. I missed Jordan and was incredibly lonely at times. I missed my mom, who had started a master's degree in my last year of high school and needed to travel to another province for several weeks at a time. I missed my brother, who had packed up one day and left town without warning. There were times I felt like the only family member left in the house we had all once shared, the only one who wasn't moving on. Nothing was keeping me chained to this city or this university.

On a crisp late summer morning, I left behind everything I knew: my family, friends, a great job and my shot at a degree. Jordan and I packed everything we could into a U-Haul trailer, and prepared to drive to Vancouver where I had been accepted into a college music program. My chest constricted as I walked out of my childhood home. So many memories were held within those walls: ones I would cherish and others I hoped to forget. Even when I visited, I would only ever be a guest; this would never be my home again.

On the driveway, my mom hugged me tightly, rocking me back and forth as she had done when I was small. I breathed in the familiar scent of her shampoo and hand lotion. Reluctantly, I pulled away, and she placed a small box wrapped in tissue paper into my hand. I peeled back the paper to reveal a jewelry box. Inside lay a Saint Christopher pendant on a gold chain.

"Saint Christopher is the patron saint of travel," she told me. "Please, be safe," she added, her voice thick with tears.

Then I climbed into the truck where Jordan was waiting, and we drove off. I waved until we were out of sight.

Those years in music school were some of the best times of my life. I remember happy and carefree times filled with friends and love; days with classmates, cramming for upcoming exams; rehearsing songs we hadn't yet learned but needed to perform in minutes; and hazy, alcohol-tinged nights out on the town. Although fighting with bureaucracy again became a frequent occurrence, it's only a vague memory.

"I'm not sure what to do," sighed the bewildered disability services coordinator as I sat in an uncomfortable chair in her stuffy office. "People with disabilities usually don't study outside of their home provinces, so the provincial governments can't seem to figure out who should pay for your educational supports, like the people we need to hire to transcribe your class materials into an accessible format."

We had many such unproductive meetings during my time there. Advocating for my education sometimes took up several hours a week, while I tried to maintain a full course load and the busy social calendar of a college student. It was thanks to the extraordinary staff of the music program, as well as the kindness of my fellow students, that I was able to graduate on time. I never did receive a single dollar of government support, despite the years of advocacy.

Although my memories of those years are bathed in a rosy glow, symptoms of mental illness began to creep back into my life. I kept myself together until my last year of college. I began missing classes. On the days I did go to school, my anxiety would make me ill.

On winter break, I went back home to Edmonton and saw my family doctor; she prescribed an antidepressant and told me to seek counselling in Vancouver. I asked a trusted friend to recommend a therapist. The psychologist he suggested was extremely compassionate, perhaps too much so. A warm, grandmotherly woman, somewhere in her mid-sixties, she seemed better suited to baking chocolate chip cookies than telling people hard truths. She expressed sympathy and validated the difficulties I was having, but didn't offer much in the way of concrete steps I could take to get better. I stopped seeing her after a short while.

Because my doctor was 1200 kilometres away, I had no follow-up discussion about how the medication was working. After about a year, I did exactly what no one should: I quit taking the pills, cold turkey. I told myself I was feeling okay; I wanted to go out with my friends without concerns about mixing alcohol with antidepressants.

I didn't seek help for a long time after that, but that's not because I was better. I was always anxious in public, constantly feeling trapped, frozen, living in fight-or-flight mode. I went through frequent bouts of severe depression, but I always managed to pull myself out of the abyss. Suicide was never far from my thoughts. Even on a good day, watching the subway pull into the station or looking down from an extreme height, I would ponder just how quickly I could end it all. These were purely idle thoughts; I knew I could never die in such ways. I wanted to die where nobody would see me. Ironically, it didn't feel right to traumatize anyone who might witness such a public act, just because *I* no longer wanted to live.

Suicidal ideation was something I always kept in my back pocket, much like one might draw comfort from a lucky penny or other memento they carry with them everywhere. Contemplating my death was like that feeling you get when you pull the covers back over yourself on a rainy, cold morning, the instant you realize it's the weekend and you have nowhere to be, or wrapping yourself in a big, fluffy towel after a hot bath. Thoughts of dying brought me feelings of peace, solace, and well-being.

Life in Lima

As the plane touched down in Lima, Peru, I felt no fear, only the weary contentment of a traveller who had finally come home after a long time away. I was about to start on the adventure that, to some degree, I always knew would be a part of my story. Although Jordan and I knew no one, had no jobs and only the possessions we could carry, I was not afraid. In fact, it was my secret hope that I would never again live in Canada.

People who knew me when I was very young told me that I always seemed to know I would leave Canada one day to live in a different country. In my opinion, Canada is not one of the developed nations to live in if you have a disability. The disability legislation is shamefully behind that of other countries with a similar economic status. Until 2018, a person with a disability who wished to immigrate to Canada could be denied on nothing more than the grounds of their disability. When the Immigration Act was amended, the backlash against allowing more people with disabilities to immigrate to Canada was disheartening.

I've grown up feeling like my country doesn't want me. It's hard for me to say I'm Canadian with any amount of pride.

After I graduated from college, Jordan and I began to make plans to leave Canada. As far back as I can remember, I have identified more with the Latino culture than the culture of Canada. Because I had grown up as immersed in the Latino Canadian community as possible, I spoke fluent Spanish. A Latin American country was the obvious choice. If we were going to make such a big move, why not move to an entirely different continent? After much discussion, we decided on Peru. There was no particular reason for our decision, but I had read a book about Peru in elementary school, and the Peruvians I knew in Canada were kind people.

We bought our plane tickets almost a year in advance so we would have an exact date to work toward. I took a course to get certified to teach English as a second language, and spent that year teaching ESL in Canada, honing my skills. We saved every penny we could, in case we didn't find jobs right away in Peru. I tearfully left Bibby with my mom in Edmonton.

Lima's airport was crowded and noisy. We made our way through customs, grabbed our bags and found the person who had come to meet us, the former neighbour of a Peruvian girl I knew in Canada. We would stay with him and his family until we found more permanent accommodations.

As we stepped out of the airport, I got my first taste of Lima's beautiful chaos. Horns honked, taxi drivers shouted, people jostled around, and everyone seemed to be in a hurry. The air smelled of engine exhaust and fried food.

As our host drove us to his home, we marvelled at the traffic. It was like nothing we had ever seen. Cars drove on every conceivable inch of the road: no one stayed in their own lane or obeyed traffic signals. The rules of the road in Lima appeared non-existent and it was every man for himself. The more drivers honked their horns, or the louder they yelled at each other, the better.

My life in Lima was a series of stark contrasts. Shortly after we arrived, we were having drinks with new friends at a sidewalk restaurant. We got word that riots had started several blocks away, and the disturbance was quickly heading in our direction.

Riots in Peru are not like the hockey riots in Canada. People get killed during Peruvian riots. Restaurant patrons scattered, abandoning food and drinks as they ran for cover. It was pandemonium. We rushed into the basement of an open church, moments before the heavy iron gates clanged shut behind us. Sitting in a small huddle of complete strangers as they sang hymns, we waited for the danger to pass. It was striking, these people singing praises to God, while people experienced violence and fear outside.

I made friends from all walks of life. I lounged poolside in mansions staffed by armies of hired help, sipped cocktails in swanky condos in upscale entertainment districts, and shared meals with people who had nothing, yet would give everything. In these latter homes, we would sit to eat on dirt floors, balancing tin plates of food on our laps because there were no tables or chairs. Bare bulbs crackled above, casting only shadowy light throughout the dank, windowless rooms.

At Christmas time, I accompanied friends into the poorest, most dangerous districts of Lima, where they had organized events for some of Lima's most underprivileged children. There was a certain heaviness in the air, an oppressive heat, mixed with the sickly sweet smell of rotting garbage, cooking food and raw sewage. All around, a cacophony of humanity: dogs barking, children playing, voices raised in anger, in laughter, in reproach. Many of these communities are built on hills, and we would hike to the top, where children would gather around a makeshift stage, drink hot chocolate from paper cups, and watch volunteer entertainers with rapt attention as they spread Christmas cheer to this vulnerable population.

Trips to these communities were not without risk. We would march purposefully together in tight knots past ramshackle shelters, their occupants eyeing us warily, or with overly keen interest. One afternoon, a group of men gathered around a pile of burning garbage stopped to stare at me. "Hey white girl!" yelled one of the men in vulgar Spanish. "Watch out for the thieves!" A peal of cold laughter rippled through the group. I kept my gaze fixed straight ahead, careful to neither speed up nor slow down, pretending complete indifference.

It struck me during these events that, until a certain age, all children are alike. Barefoot and clothed in dirty rags, tots clung to the legs of their mothers—exhausted young women not much more than children themselves. Yet, these kids exuded the same childlike trust and hopefulness as the children from affluent families I knew in Canada. They all cried and laughed for the same things, they all sought a place of love and safety. In a small way, they reminded me of my early blissful years, when I felt safe in the certainty of knowing my place in the world. It wouldn't be long before the harsh reality of their existence would catch up to them. They would grow to understand that many people had much more than they did. Soon, they would know the dangers that surrounded them; although, supported by their culture, most would grow into contented and positive adults despite the hardships. But, for this fleeting time, they knew no different. They were like any other wide-eyed, innocent children, dazzled by the magic of Christmas.

Although there are exceptions to the rule, Canadians tend to have one of two responses to my blindness. They either studiously avoid the topic to the point of discomfort, or they try to pretend they're totally cool with it by constantly cracking jokes. Don't get me wrong, I like a good blind joke as much as the next person, but they're no longer funny when you've heard them a thousand times before. People are far less original than they think.

In contrast, Peruvians, and Latinos in general, tend to be far less fazed. Without making a big deal, they easily anticipate my needs. They ask fewer questions, but observe much more. They don't discourage me from trying something new in fear that I might get hurt. You want to climb a pyramid? Set off fireworks? Drive a quad? Sure, why the hell not? They handle it all so casually, but not with the forced casualness of many Canadians.

While skeptics ask if my total inclusion in Latin society was because I'm white, I would suggest it runs deeper than that. It wasn't until many years after returning from Peru that Eduardo, my best friend from Mexico, provided the most likely explanation.

"Why do you think it's so easy for people in Latin America to accept me, to not question my abilities like so many Canadians?" I asked him as we sat in the tall grass on his family's farm in Querétaro, Mexico.

He didn't hesitate. "In the Latin culture, family and friends are the most important thing," he said. "We want everyone to feel a part of the group, you know? Of course you should do the same things as we're all doing, and we shouldn't think twice about it. You belong, you're part of us. That you feel included is more important than any silly fears or preconceptions. It's not something we even think about really. I mean, it's weird to consider that you wouldn't just do the same things as we're doing if you want to."

Having no background in linguistics, I've always wondered if a part of this easy acceptance also stems from the Spanish language itself. Spanish is a more descriptive language than English; we only need look at how much longer a text in Spanish is in comparison to its English equivalent. This helps Spanish-speaking people provide me with better verbal explanations. As well, many of the nicknames given to friends and family have to do with the physical attributes of an individual. Nicknames like *Little Fatty*, *Old Man* or *White Girl* don't sound quite so endearing in English, but are commonly used in Spanish. While some may find this offensive, to me, it removes the elephant in the room, giving voice to what everyone is thinking. By calling a spade a spade, we can get past our differences, and quickly move on to what makes us all human.

After living with an incredibly kind and generous family for a few months, we moved to a middle-class district in Lima. It was more central to our jobs as English teachers. We rented a room from a single mother of a young son with severe learning disabilities. There was no money to send the boy to a private school, and public schools were unable to meet his needs. With few options, his mother would leave him at home for hours while she went to work, locking the door to ensure he didn't wander off. There were no books or television, no phone and no contact with the outside world. He could watch the world pass by from his bedroom window.

Poverty can breed desperation, sometimes leading good people to do dishonest things. When we were introduced to our landlady by one of her coworkers, it was clear she saw us as the means to a better life for her and her son. She used our rent money to do extensive renovations on the apartment. One day, without warning, we came home to find the place was no longer habitable. We had suddenly become homeless in Peru.

There are few things in life more humbling than standing on the doorstep of a complete stranger with all your worldly possessions at your feet. The brother of a friend of a friend from Canada took us in without questions when we had nowhere left to go. There is nothing more beautiful than the compassion and generosity of strangers. It is a lesson I will carry with me forever; one, I hope, that will dictate how I treat others in their hour of need.

Life in Peru was full of what I like to think of as "character-building" experiences. One Saturday night, suffering from a kidney infection, I was taken to a private hospital by two friends who worked there. When we arrived, I quickly realized it was unlike any hospital in Canada. As we pulled up outside the emergency doors of the impressively modern building, a team of nurses was waiting with a wheelchair, and I was taken directly into an examination room.

Jordan, who still spoke little Spanish, watched helplessly as nurses immediately began to stick needles in me, giving me antibiotics and hooking me up to an IV.

This was our first experience with private healthcare and he figured, if they were working so quickly, it must mean I was gravely ill. The friends who accompanied us could offer him little reassurance. They had arrived with a carload of people we didn't know, and no one in the group spoke English. Having come directly from a party, the festive atmosphere persisted while my friends and their friends waited; they laughed loudly and raced wheelchairs up and down the empty halls. In Peru, the party must go on, even if someone needs to go to the emergency room.

There was also the time we became stranded for two days in a remote mountain village, where we had gone to visit a friend who had moved there for work. Loading into a fifteen-passenger van in Lima, we began what was supposed to be a four-hour trip to our friend's new village. The van's driver had clearly not consulted a map, and as night fell, we were lost on treacherous one-lane mountain roads. Frustrated, the driver began to drive more and more recklessly; passengers reminded him that his wife and son were also in the vehicle, hoping to convince him to slow down. There was a sheer cliff on one side with no guardrail. One tiny slip of a wheel and we could plummet to our deaths. They would likely never find our bodies. The road was so narrow that, if we got out of the van, we were likely to be hit by a mining truck. I wondered if I should make some final calls, just in case, but then I remembered that we had lost cellphone reception hours before.

Miraculously, we finally arrived at our friend's village in the dead of night. To our dismay, we were told we were actually to stay at a place fifteen minutes back down the mountain. A hot meal was waiting for us there. The van driver flatly refused to drive even a minute more, so our friend scrambled in search of a place where we could all stay. In the end, we spread thin blankets over the bare wooden floor of an abandoned house to sleep. High in the Andean mountains, nights are freezing, and we had no food or water.

In the light of morning, things seemed more promising. The quaint village was incredibly picturesque, like a still-inhabited Machu Picchu, but without the tourists. Stone houses with thatched roofs dotted the landscape, and crystal-clear streams burbled under the bluest of skies. Alpacas and other livestock were led down cobblestone streets by Quechuan natives, stocky people made strong by hard labour in the cold and harsh landscape. Most of the villagers were older, the younger ones having gone to Lima in search of work. A few younger women carried produce or babies on their backs.

Refreshed from a night's sleep, the driver of the van agreed to take us back down the mountain to where we were supposed to be staying, but he soon discovered that the van wouldn't start because of the extreme altitude. The men of the village gathered around the vehicle, calling out suggestions to no avail. A few workers, passing through in a mining truck, agreed to take us to the next village. Most of our group piled into the truck bed, holding on for dear life as we made our way at breakneck speed down the narrow, steep and twisting incline. "Holy shit!" Jordan yelled over the sound of the truck's engine and the rushing wind, "I literally think we're gonna die! I'm gonna get a picture of that cliff, just in case we live. Nobody would believe this." He clung to the side of the truck with one hand while he quickly snapped a photo with the other.

When we reached the next village, we received word that the van had finally started and the driver had immediately left for Lima. He was supposed to take us back with him the following day; our little group was left stranded in the mountains.

The "excellent" accommodations had been grossly oversold. Another abandoned house awaited us. Perched on stilts, it reminded me of one of my childhood tree forts. The whole structure swayed when the wind blew, and there was still no food or running water. The elderly woman who owned the place was in failing health. When a girl from our group shyly asked if there was somewhere to take a shower, she was incredulous. "Of course! You shower in the river." The river was also where the toilets emptied after being manually flushed using a pail of water from a nearby stream.

No one has ever died from not showering for a few days.

After another chilly night, spent on a cot that smelled of kerosene, the friend we'd come to visit asked if I would sing at his church. There were no instruments anywhere to be found but, ironically, I had brought my computer; and although there was no internet, we managed to come up with a backing track I could sing to that morning. I stood on a stage carved out of earth and sang to the most appreciative little congregation, some of whom had walked hours from faraway villages. The gentle lowing of nearby cattle accompanied me, and stray dogs wandered in and out of the open sides of the stone building.

After church, the entire village gathered to share a meal. The people of the village ate only what they could grow, hunt or fish, there being no store for miles.

By late afternoon, Jordan and I decided to try to head back to Lima alone. Another mining truck took us part of the way down the mountain to a larger village, where buses passed through a few times a day. We waited for hours in the rain on the village's only street, while people stared down at us curiously from second-story windows. A few buses drove by, all full. Finally, as it was getting dark, we paid someone with a car an exorbitant amount of money to take us farther down the mountain to yet another, larger village. After waiting well into the night, a bus bound for Lima finally arrived. We climbed aboard, feeling immensely relieved. That is, until the bus broke down two hours into the journey.

As time passed, our money dwindled. With our Peruvian salaries, I eventually had to accept that we were one emergency away from being unable to eat. Jordan continued to struggle daily with the language and culture.

And so, I did the most heart-wrenching thing I have ever done. I booked plane tickets back to Canada.

Our last weekend in Lima could not have been more beautiful. Practically all of our friends stayed the last two nights at the home of an extremely hospitable couple, friends who put us up after our apartment lease expired a few days earlier. By Saturday, a large group had gathered; one friend even travelled five hours by bus through the jungle to say goodbye. That night, in one of Lima's entertainment districts, I experienced some of the most profound joy I had ever known. As our large group crowded around a number of tables in a restaurant, I listened to the lively conversations going on around me, and my heart swelled, knowing that everyone was there because of us; our friendship had meant something to them. After we finished eating, we headed to an enormous park in the middle of the city. There, under the flickering yellow light of kerosene lanterns, with the heavy scent of deep-fried food in the warm air, we danced together with reckless abandon to the cries of street vendors, the sizzle of food cooking on their carts, and live music playing in the distance.

The next morning, we all got up late, tired from the previous night's festivities. In true Peruvian fashion, we spent the afternoon working together to make a giant meal to be enjoyed that evening. We made all my favourite Peruvian dishes, accompanied by Peruvian drinks and snacks I loved and would miss. I don't think

I have ever felt more love than I did in that room that night, as we all ate together one last time.

After the meal, everyone gathered round. Each person talked about Jordan and me, and what our friendship had meant to them. Even the four-year-old sister of the host had something to say. One friend was crying so hard he was unable to finish his speech. I held him as my own tears began to fall, and wondered how leaving this place of love and belonging would ever be okay.

What I knew I'd always remember most about that year in Peru were the small things. A drink and conversation shared with a friend, nights spent listening to Peruvian music in Lima's parks, feeling a joyous sense of belonging in ways I never had in Canada. The year I spent in Peru was the best I have known. I was more *me* during that year than I have ever been, a larger, more defined version of myself.

The following day, Jordan and I took care of the boring intricacies of our return to Canada. I watched the clock inch toward 7:00 PM, when we would need to leave for the airport. I wanted time to last forever, yet I also wanted to get the painful goodbye over with. On that final night in Lima, I sat between two dear friends in the back seat and held on to them with everything I had. I knew that as soon as I let go, it would all be over. As the lights of Lima flashed by outside the car window, I said a silent goodbye to the city that had become more my home than Canada would ever be.

At the airport, I clung to my friends. I wish I could remember every last word we shared. Then I let them go. While in the security line, I turned back to them one last time before a wall separated us from view. As the plane took off, I watched the pinprick lights of the city below grow smaller and smaller as we rose into the night sky.

Our first interaction upon arrival in Canada was with a man in the airport who asked Jordan what was wrong with me. Had I been born "like that?" He didn't even have the courtesy to address me directly. My heart broke. During the entire year I'd spent in Peru, I had not once been treated with such disrespect. Within five minutes of being back in Canada, I was reminded of exactly why I had wanted to leave.

Island Life

For a month after returning from Peru, I struggled just to get out of bed. I did little more than chat online with my friends in Lima. I could not come to terms with the reverse culture shock. Jordan and I had hoped to pick up where we'd left off, but we soon realized we could no longer afford to live in the beautiful, but incredibly expensive, city of Vancouver. We accepted defeat. With the prospect of work and a lower cost of living, we got out of our apartment lease, packed up our instruments, clothes and a few pieces of secondhand furniture, and took the two-hour ferry ride to our new home on Vancouver Island.

I gradually settled into my new life. I got involved in music again, gigging as much as I could. Putting my passion for animals into action, I volunteered daily for a cat rescue group and, with fond memories of horseback riding at a friend's ranch near Vancouver, I leased a horse to ride once a week.

In time, I overcame a terrible case of songwriter's block and turned my experiences in Peru into songs. I hired some of my favourite musicians from across Canada and we came together in a studio on Vancouver Island to record a new album. It was a whirlwind few weeks. The message of my experiences seemed to be universal. The new songs received airplay on independent radio stations, and were nominated for awards, and won. I could not have been more grateful for the positive reception after what had been a long musical hiatus.

Because of the lack of infrastructure where we now lived, I struggled to be independent. There were very few buses, and even if there had been, there really was nowhere to go. I found it extremely difficult to meet people and make friends, and my self-worth began to plummet. I was sick of feeling like I owed people, that they gave more to our relationship than I did, and thus were "superior." I wanted a strong, independent self-identity. I wanted to come together with Jordan at night and talk about our day, but I craved my own self outside of the life we shared. There were very few decisions I could make independently, and I felt myself being absorbed into those around me, no longer my own entity.

I had a few good friends close by, including Chelsea, my best friend since childhood. A number of years after I returned from Peru, my mom took a job on the island, and several aunts and uncles also moved closer to me. But no matter how many loved ones I surrounded myself with, I still wasn't meeting my own needs. I felt utterly alone.

A few years after moving to the island, Jordan and I opened our own business, effectively creating jobs for ourselves. We did the typical things expected of adults, ending up with a mortgage, a car payment and little ambition. That 'me'-ness I had found in Peru slipped away almost unnoticeably, until it was nearly too late.

One Year Earlier

My depressive episodes were becoming more and more frequent and lasting longer and longer. In November of 2018, I entered into one such period that seemed endless. I got sicker as the months passed. I withdrew from friends and loved ones, I turned my phone off for days at a time, refusing to answer calls or texts. I completely stopped playing music. By early summer, I had mostly stopped eating, almost never slept, and my hair was falling out. I prayed for something, anything just to make it all stop. By that point, I would have taken anything I was offered. I was so tired, all I craved was oblivion. I wanted nothing more than to die, but I didn't have the energy to do anything about it.

I knew I was near the point of no return when I woke up one morning in late June. I didn't have much time left to help myself. I made an emergency doctor's appointment. As I sat, shaking uncontrollably in a tiny exam room with a doctor I'd never met before, I gathered the last of my strength and asked him to please help me.

Doctor Austin's first step was to have me complete two psychological assessments, the PHQ-9 and GAD-7, questionnaires that measure the severity of depression and anxiety, respectively. My scores were extremely high on both.

"Would you be open to trying medication?" he asked. I nodded, willing to try anything by that point.

After asking me about my history of antidepressant use, the doctor sat for a few minutes, deliberating over which medication to try. He made a thoughtful selection, and scheduled a follow-up appointment in one week's time. Although I told him I planned to hire a private counsellor, Doctor Austin put my name on the long waiting list for a public health therapist. "The more support you can get, the better your outcome will be," he said.

He seemed to have a keen interest in mental health and didn't dismiss my concerns as I feared he might. At the end of the appointment, he said, "If you have any concerns at all, or if things get worse, please come back in. I'll see you right away. And if you feel like you can't keep yourself safe, don't hesitate to go to the hospital."

Ending up in the hospital had been my greatest fear throughout the years of struggling with my mental health, so I brushed off his advice. The hospital was for other people, not me. I thought I'd rather die than go through the shame of being admitted to a psych ward.

The first couple of weeks on the new antidepressant were hell. I was constantly nauseated and had even less energy than before. I persevered, knowing that not taking it was no longer an option and bit by bit, the unpleasant side effects faded.

One evening—a few weeks after my first appointment with Doctor Austin—Bibby, by then fifteen and long since retired from her guide dog duties, began to have repetitive seizures. She had been healthy and spry for her age, and it seemed the worst kind of injustice; this graceful, poised creature could no longer control her own body and had no understanding of what was happening to her. She had had a few seizures before, the cause of which remained a mystery to her veterinarians, but that night, the seizures were continuous. Each time she seized, she was slower to come out of it. It was clear they were weakening her.

A call to an emergency vet provided little hope. We could wait until the morning to have her regular vet euthanize her, but we'd be running the risk that she would suffer greatly, or we could take her in that night to be put to sleep. She was the last creature on Earth who deserved to suffer a minute longer than absolutely necessary.

Since she could no longer walk unaided, Jordan gently carried her in her bed to the car for her final journey. The sun had set, and the last hues were fading from the sky as my mom and I sat in the back seat with Bibby. I asked Jordan to drive past the ocean where my companion had loved to walk. I wanted her to see it one last time.

As we drove slowly by, Bibby struggled to sit up, picking up the scent of the salty, summer ocean breeze through the open window. She sighed in the way she always did when everything was right in her world.

When we arrived at the darkened veterinary hospital, Bibby managed to get shakily to her feet. As was her custom, she was going to do this her own way. She stopped to sniff the flowers growing along the walkway to the doors. A soft rain began to fall, rejuvenating the parched summer earth; the raindrops mingled with the tears on our faces. Then, as best she could, Bibby drew herself up. With her head held high, she proudly took her final steps into the vet's office.

A heavily pregnant, soft-spoken young vet gave Bibby a thorough examination. "I can send her to Vancouver for testing if you want," she told us, "but that's a long trip and I don't believe the test results will change the outcome. When a dog this old has seizures like the ones Bibby is having, it's not good news. There is really nothing more we can do for her."

It was time to let her go.

We all sat on the floor with her where she lay in her bed. As the vet injected a sedative, Bibby sighed and closed her eyes, letting her head come to rest on my lap as she had done during so many bus rides on bitterly cold mornings, long university lectures, and plane rides to new and exciting places. She slept so peacefully, the fear and confusion of the past hours were gone. We held her for a while longer and talked to her as she slept, our tears soaking her once glossy black fur, now slightly dulled with age. I ran my hands over her sleeping form, forever committing to memory the contours of her body, once as familiar to me as my own. When the vet gave her the final injection to stop her heart, she quietly slipped away.

"She's gone, I'm so sorry," said the vet softly, turning away to compose herself. She didn't need to tell me. You cannot work so intimately with another being and not sense the moment they leave this Earth.

In a strange way, Bibby's death helped me wake up, to step outside of the misery I had been cloaked in for so long. I felt guilty that, in her final months, I had been so wrapped up in myself that I barely acknowledged her, or anyone else for that matter. Her death showed me it was time for me to start living again.

As painful as the change would be, I knew we could no longer stay in the small town we'd been living in for the past several years. Jordan was working away more often, and I needed to be in a bigger city with accessible transportation. In the space of only a few weeks, we had chosen a new city on the island, a few hours away; we sold our house and bought another.

The first months in the new city were terrifying. After relying on others to drive me everywhere for so long, being out in public by myself again was so stressful as to be nearly impossible. If I knew I was going to be taking the bus somewhere, I would get so sick that I couldn't eat the day before or the day of the bus ride. I was obsessed with perfection; afraid I would stumble or take a step in the wrong direction. What would others think? I wanted everyone to be comfortable around me, and for people to see me as wholly independent and capable. I persevered and, bit by bit, being alone in public got easier.

During the long months of recovery from my major depressive episode, my small circle of loved ones walked beside me every step of my journey back to the land of the living. I booked a trip to visit some of my closest friends in Mexico, and began recording music in Spanish with a producer from Cuba—a long-held dream of mine. With medical intervention, the support of people who loved me, and the prospect of exciting things to come, I began to get better—slowly but surely.

And then, in March of 2020, the COVID-19 pandemic hit.

Preparing to Die

I sat on the couch in my living room with the blinds drawn, numbly listening to yet another news briefing on the COVID-19 pandemic. Case numbers were rising, people were dying, and it showed no signs of letting up. Because of the government-imposed lockdown measures to control the spread of COVID-19, soon it would be two entire months since I had seen a single person apart from Jordan.

I had been able to manage my depression for the past several months, mostly. I set long-term survival goals. For example: *I can't kill myself until I finish this amazing recording project I'm working on*; or, *I can't kill myself until my friend Eduardo comes to visit in August*; or, *I can't kill myself until I see my friends in Mexico one last time.*

In December of 2019, I had seen a specialist to have a long-awaited genetic test done. It would tell me the exact gene mutation that caused my blindness; we would then know how to potentially treat it. I'd been hearing about this possibility since I was old enough to understand language. Family and doctors alike had hoped that one day such a test would be available to me. The most accurate test was being conducted in a laboratory in California. It was prohibitively expensive for Canadians until the provincial government finally agreed to pay for it in 2019. I had a DNA sample taken in Vancouver and sent to the United States for testing.

There are currently 25 gene mutations known to cause my eye condition. Of those genes, there is treatment available for only one of them. The specialist warned me that there was an approximately 30 percent chance that the test would come back inconclusive if I had a gene mutation that had not yet been mapped. If the test came back with a match, there was a good chance it would not be the gene for which there was a treatment.

If, however, I had that one treatable gene mutation, I would have to make a hard decision. Most sighted people believe the answer is obvious, but as with most things in life, it's not that black and white. The surgery presents risks. There's no guarantee of success. Oh... and it costs 800,000 US dollars! Even if I could come up with the money, would I want to? I would have to relearn so many things. My brain would be overwhelmed by visual stimuli that it never had to process before. Would I want to change so drastically? Should I feel that I needed to?

Whether or not to restore sight to a blind person is an intensely personal decision. Some blind people would love to see, because they're interested in what the world looks like and/or how their lives would be more convenient. They also know that, as a sighted person, they would face less discrimination. Other people like how they are and see no reason to change, believing the world must change, not them. Although I honestly cannot say if I'd choose to have my sight restored no matter the cost or the risk, I tend to fall more in the first camp. Although I don't much care to see the colours of a sunset or what my loved ones look like, the inconveniences of blindness cannot be denied. Whatever this test told me, I knew it would bring up a lot of complicated feelings.

The results of my genetic test would take approximately six months to come in, so a follow-up appointment was scheduled for June of 2020. A big survival tactic for me became *I can't kill myself until I know my test results.* However, when the pandemic hit, all my goals were put on hold. Would I even get my test results in June? I no longer knew if or when the things I'd been looking forward to would happen, and what was the point of living without attainable goals?

I began to obsessively follow the news about COVID, reading into everything that was said, praying we'd have answers soon. My doctors and therapists had stopped seeing patients in person and became harder to reach. Because the few appointments we had were over the phone, they couldn't see the physical signs of my decline—how exhausted I looked and how thin I'd become. If they had, perhaps they could have intervened. Maybe they could have prevented what was coming.

My therapist, Chris, sounded worried. "I've made you an appointment with a psychiatrist," he told me in what I believed would be our last session. "I made it on an urgent basis, but even then, because of COVID, the earliest I could schedule you is mid-July."

It was mid-May.

Before he hung up, he implored me to go to the hospital if things got worse. "I need to wrap this up," he said at the end of the session, sounding like there was much more he wanted to say. "I can't make you go, but please, if necessary, please remember to go to the hospital." He briefly explained the process I would undergo if I were to end up in the ER and then hung up.

That afternoon, I called Doctor Austin's office and made a phone appointment. I planned to plead with him to give me something to get me through until… until when? When would things get better? I didn't really know what I wanted him to do for me. I waited for my phone to ring at the scheduled time, but the call didn't come. When it finally came hours later, I didn't hear the phone ring. I did not call to reschedule. I had given up. I knew I had little hope of making it to that psychiatrist appointment in two months.

I had actively begun planning to die.

From research I had conducted on and off over the past several years, I would construct an exit bag—a large bag that is fastened around the head and allows an inert gas to flow into it. With the use of an inert gas, there is none of the panic or struggle typically associated with asphyxiation. Unconsciousness comes quickly, followed by death shortly after. An advantage to this method is that there is little time for a change of heart in someone who really wants to die.

While I could easily obtain most of the necessary supplies, the tank of gas was going to be a problem. I worried that stores wouldn't sell it to me without a good reason, and even if they did, I could hardly take it home on the bus. If by some miracle I managed to buy it and bring it home, I needed a place to store it where it wouldn't be found. Because inert gases are used in specific trades, I hoped to find a tradesperson who would buy it for me. There were stipulations. It had to be someone who would never find out afterwards, someone who could never be traced. It needed to be someone who wouldn't be in town long. But, because of the pandemic, this obstacle was going to be next to impossible to overcome.

The only feeling worse than desperately wanting to die is desperately wanting to die with no clear way out.

Another plan started to take shape. In the trial and error I had undergone with various medications over the past year, without really considering why, I had held on to the extra antidepressants, anti-anxiety medications and sleep aids I'd been prescribed. I looked up lethal doses and, by my calculations, I would have more than enough. I knew the statistics. Suicide by overdose is not a sure way to die; in fact, it is largely unsuccessful. However, I figured that, with enough pills, alcohol and time, I could pull it off. My worst fear was ending up in the hospital having my stomach pumped, but I'd gotten desperate. Having sufficient time would be easy if I planned it right, but I needed to ensure the medications and alcohol stayed in my system and that I didn't vomit. I figured I could accomplish this by taking a large dose of antiemetics shortly before the lethal medications. This method would be messier and more uncertain, but I felt a great sense of relief now that I had a plan. The only question now was "When?"

During the past year, I had lost contact with a lot of my friends. Very few people saw my struggles; but those who glimpsed my depression had markedly different responses. Some got angry, because anger is so closely tied to fear. Others tried to convince me to make promises I didn't know if I could keep. There were others who vowed to be there night or day, but they had no clue what to say, and really, how could they? Others couldn't stand to speak of it—my pain was too much for them to bear. But in the end, when it all came to light, the most common refrain was, "But you always seemed so happy."

As my illness progressed, Jordan took on more and more of my responsibilities, both in our business and at home. His solid presence was comforting, but I knew the severity of my depression scared him. A self-proclaimed "doer," I sensed his anguish at not being able to fix things for me. He desperately wanted to help me find the will to live, but as far as I was concerned, he was looking for solutions to problems that were unsolvable.

Apart from my aunt, an ER doctor who had seen it all, the only other person I could talk to freely about my suicidal thoughts was Eduardo. Months earlier, shortly after my first meeting with Doctor Austin, Eduardo listened as I told him the terrible truth. He didn't get angry or react with fear, disgust or shock.

Eduardo spoke words of comfort I will never forget. "I truly hope that there never comes a day when you're not here," he said gently. "You're an important part of my life, and you have so much more life to live, so many things to do still. There's your next trip to Mexico, my next visit to Canada, so many songs left to learn, to write and to play. You still need to teach me to play the piano and to help me with my English, remember? There are so many memories you still need to make, and I have faith in you. You are so loved. You've shown me such a special part of who you are, and you are needed here."

For a brief moment, as my friend spoke of happy future memories yet to be made, I could imagine myself living them. He made me feel I still had something to offer this world and the people in it. He told me that he believed depression came largely from not feeling useful; although I'd never thought of it like that before, he was right. I was grateful to have a friend from whom I didn't need to hide the truth. He accepted it all with compassion and grace.

I wouldn't learn until much later how much it hurt him to be there for me in that way.

In the last weeks of May, the COVID-19 quarantine rules relaxed slightly, and I was finally able to see Chelsea, my best friend since childhood, who now also lived on the island. From joyful times spent making mix CDs for epic dance parties in my basement, to the beginning of my battle with depression, Chelsea had been there and seen it all.

I remember very little of the time I spent with her that day. I only know we went furniture shopping so I could use a store credit that was about to expire. I bought a chair and a picture of a bedazzled tabby cat that we both found hilarious. I remember this clearly because the purchases are still in my home. Although I was happy to see Chelsea after the period of time that the quarantine had kept us apart, the rest of that day remains a blank, as do most of the days leading up to my hospitalization.

My mother also stopped by that week, to deliver food I would never eat. Although they didn't know what I was planning, after not seeing me for months, my mom and Chelsea both clearly saw how I had deteriorated. I had hidden the truth so well for so long. I'd grown up on the stage after all, and every performer knows the number one rule of the stage: No matter what happens, never let them see you're afraid. Now, however, the physical evidence of my illness could no longer be disguised with carefully chosen clothes or makeup. I was rail thin, my ribs showed, and my hip bones jutted out at sharp angles. I looked depleted. The light had gone from my eyes. My hands shook constantly, a result of starvation and of the combination of meds I was taking. Every day, I was using my "as needed" anti-anxiety medication at the maximum daily dose allowed. It numbed the panic just enough to make me feel desolate.

Each night when I went to bed, I would pray to God, the universe or whoever the hell was out there listening to not let me wake up again. Every morning when I opened my eyes, I was disappointed that my prayer had not been answered.

During those final weeks, knowing how utterly unfair I was being, I asked Jordan to let me die. I pleaded for his understanding and begged for his blessing. "I can't… I just can't," he said over and over again, shattered.

I was conscious of the strain I was putting on my loved ones. Part of me wanted them to leave, and part of me was terrified they would. I hated myself enough (and loved them too much), to keep putting them through this. I would be the one to leave.

The week before I planned to die, I texted my aunt, the ER doctor, to ask about support groups for loved ones of people with mental illness. In retrospect, I suppose I was asking her where they could turn for support after I was gone. She texted back, asking if she could call me.

Over the phone, I told her as much of the truth as I could manage. "Honestly," she said kindly, "if you were a patient of mine, I would say the hospital was where you needed to be."

I asked her what it would be like there, and she spent a long time explaining the intake process to me, answering my questions with clarity and honesty. "You might see and hear some hard things. There may be people in restraints." In a strange way, I think it was her complete honesty that helped me take the next step. If she had glossed over the hard parts, I might never have gone to the hospital.

"You don't have to go tonight," she said. "You can take a bit of time to get ready, then decide on a day to go." I was relieved that she wasn't pushing me into something I didn't yet feel prepared for.

That night, I made a decision, an unspoken promise to myself and my loved ones. I would take the weekend to prepare, either for hospitalization or death, and on Monday, I would go to the hospital. If I wasn't admitted, or if I didn't feel any better when I got out, I would waste no time. As soon as I could, I would enact my plan to die.

On Sunday, I summoned one final burst of energy to take care of the details of death. I wrote my last will and testament. Although there wasn't time to make it legal, Jordan would automatically get all of my assets, so it didn't really matter if the document wasn't signed and witnessed. I left small things to my loved ones— sentimental tokens to remind them of me. I planned my funeral in excruciating detail. The fewer decisions I left for others to make, the better. I explained what I wanted done with my body. I asked for forgiveness I knew I didn't deserve.

I hope there's a way to find peace and to forgive me, I wrote. Every single person did more than enough. I know that thought may cross your minds, that if you'd done more, things would have been different. It was an illness, and I lost the battle with it and it was my choice and only mine in the end. Please don't think this was the easy way out, nothing about this is easy. My heart breaks for every single one of you and for the hurt and betrayal I've caused. They say that when someone dies like this, their pain isn't lost but only transferred onto the people left behind. Please know my sorrow at putting you through this. There aren't words to say how sorry I am.

For the few people closest to me, I recorded messages they would receive after I was gone. In my own way, I had been saying goodbye for weeks, but I figured maybe they'd want to hear from me one last time. Perhaps I could provide them with even the tiniest shred of closure. Much of what I told them was logistical, tying up loose ends I didn't want to leave undone. I didn't try to stop my tears. I mentioned a few of my favourite memories of them, even managing to laugh a little as I reminisced. I thanked them for all they'd done, reiterating that they could not, and should not, have done any more than they had to help me. Then, I told them I loved them and said goodbye.

The thought of any of my loved ones finding my body was excruciating. I planned to attach a note to the door, instructing them not to enter, but to call the police. I hoped with all my heart they would do as I asked.

I spent the rest of the day organizing my things, wanting them to be easy to sort through. I could not stop crying. I felt so afraid. Of the hospital, of dying, of everything. I didn't want to die alone, but my decision left me with no other choice.

Jordan tried to get me to eat a little, and I no longer had the strength to argue. I vomited immediately after. My body had stopped being able to handle solid food weeks ago.

Exhausted from the day's effort, I crawled into my bed for what I knew could be the last time. My cat, Maya, curled up in her usual spot against my stomach, purring me to sleep. I was going to miss her.

PART II:
ISLAND GENERAL HOSPITAL

Day One

I awaken early from a restless, drug-induced sleep, the first light of dawn creeping into my bedroom. The despair that has been my constant companion for so long is gone; in its place is a grim determination. Going to the hospital is the last thing left to do, my final promise. The one good thing I can say about myself is that I keep my promises.

I'm going to the hospital with no intention or real desire to get better; I simply want absolution. After I'm gone, I want people to look back on my last days and know I did what I could to fight this illness. I hope that in some way, fulfilling this last promise will make it easier for the ones I love to forgive my unforgivable act.

I manage to take a shower, something that had otherwise been impossible for me to do as of late, but I suppose I still have a bit of pride left. I dress and throw an extra change of clothes and a toothbrush in a bag. I figure it's all I'll need; I expect I might be held for 24 hours at most.

Everything is in place for when I get out of the hospital, all that's left is to pull the metaphorical trigger. I know I will likely be monitored by loved ones after coming home, but that won't last. They can't watch me 24/7. What's a few more days anyway when I've been alive for this long? The hospital will only be a minor inconvenience.

I ask Jordan to drive me to the ER. "Okay," he says, and I hear so much relief in that one small word. We leave early; I want this over with. In the car, we don't speak. What is there left to say.

At the doors of emergency, we are stopped by a screener who asks why we're here. Because of the COVID-19 pandemic, they are extremely cautious about who they allow into the hospital.

"I'm going to kill myself," I tell her matter-of-factly. During COVID-19, no family members are allowed in emergency at this hospital, but they make an exception so Jordan can escort me. I check in at the desk and repeat the reason for my visit; I hand over my ID and health card, and am given a hospital bracelet. They hand my ID back to Jordan and tell him to hold on to it for safekeeping.

We are led down a series of hallways until we arrive at a separate part of the emergency department, where people experiencing serious, acute mental health crises are held. The locked doors lead into a common room with chairs and tables bolted to the floor. A few patients are sitting, watching TV. Jordan and I sit down and I try to focus on the show that's playing, but am immediately distracted by a disturbance.

"What are you going to do, lock me up again? Abuse me?" a woman yells at a nurse.

She continues to hurl likely unfounded accusations until the nurse raises her voice as well, warning the woman that she needs to calm down. I can't breathe. Is this what this place is like? I want to run but there's nowhere to go, the doors have locked behind us. Jordan squeezes my hand and I squeeze back, holding on for dear life.

After a few minutes, the same crisis nurse approaches and introduces herself as Barb. She leads me into a small room with a glass door, two chairs and a low table, and sits down across from me. Jordan waits in the common room.

"Why are you here?" she asks.

"I'm going to kill myself," I answer again without emotion. How many times am I going to get asked this same question?

"Why?" she wants to know.

"Because everything is too much and I can't fix it and things aren't going to get better. Because I can't keep on like this. Because everything is too uncertain, and COVID has taken away the things I relied on to keep living. Because complete strangers see me and they automatically dismiss me as incapable and stupid, some have even told me they would kill themselves if they had my life. How do you live like this day in and day out and not start to believe it? I just need it all to stop."

"Did you ever think that maybe when they say these things, they're complementing your strength?" she asks.

The familiar despair comes rushing back. Even in here, they don't fucking get it.

"No," I answer flatly.

She asks if I have a plan for how I will die, and then asks for all the details of my initial plan, then the one I'd settled on out of necessity. The whole time I am deadpan, reciting words that seem to come from someone else. I don't cry, even as we discuss the final wishes I've laid out in hopes of making things easier for the ones I'm going to leave behind.

"Any history of suicide attempts?" I tell her the truth; I'm too lost to come up with a lie to get me out of this.

She takes me back to the common room and tells me to wait and that she'll page an emergency doctor who will decide the next steps.

Hours pass until she finally returns. "There's still no doctor available, the ER is packed with trauma patients right now," she explains. "The psychiatrists have already done rounds earlier today, maybe you can come back tomorrow. There are no beds downstairs and you'll have a rough night here in the psych ER." I don't know what she means by "downstairs," but I know that if I walk out of here now, I'll never come back.

"It'll be the doctor's decision," she says, and leaves me to wait once more.

I curl up in a chair, let my hair fall across my face and bury my head in my arms, trying to block it all out—the opening and closing of the heavy, automatically-locking doors, the patient complaining that they should call his dad who's a doctor, well, sort of almost a doctor. "And this is why I don't do acid anymore," he laments.

Finally, I'm roused from my stupor by a kind, young ER doctor. Her gentleness is comforting, reminding me of my aunt. We go back into the little room with the glass door and she asks me the same questions and I repeat the same answers.

"All right," she finally says, "you're going to be admitted for tonight, and you'll talk to the psychiatrist tomorrow morning."

She will now complete my first certificate. A person who is certified under British Columbia's Mental Health Act can be held in a hospital or psychiatric facility for up to 48 hours if they are believed to be a serious risk to themselves or others. Only a physician is able to certify a patient, and it is typically used only as a last resort. Many people who come to the emergency room suffering from a mental health crisis are able to go home after a session with a crisis nurse.

I return to the common room and nurse Barb comes over to Jordan and me. "Okay, you're being admitted," she says. "So, you," she nods toward Jordan, "have to leave." He fights hard not to cry. I hate myself for what I've done to him. Barb softens and says, "I'll give you a few minutes."

This goodbye needs to be quick or I'm going to fall to pieces. Every fibre of my being is screaming at me to follow him out of here, but it's too late, I am no longer free to leave. I feel trapped. Only now does it fully occur to me that I'm no longer in control. I can't believe this is truly happening. I've come to the end of the road.

Jordan is ushered out, and the door swings quickly closed behind him—with a dull thud of metal and a click as the lock engages. He is gone.

I text Chelsea and Eduardo to let them know I've been admitted into psychiatric care. Neither is surprised; in fact, it comes as a relief to them. They are part of the select few who saw this coming. I know it weighed heavily on them as they helplessly watched me become less and less able to help myself.

Moments later, a woman from the hospital pharmacy comes to talk to me about my current medications. Shortly after she leaves, nurse Barb returns and asks if I want to stay in the common room or if I'd prefer to have her take me to my room. There's a softness to her now that wasn't there before. I'm tired of listening to Acid Guy drone on about nothing to a girl who seems as shell-shocked as I feel, and I just want to be away from it all.

My room is much what I imagine a jail cell to be like, except there's no steel door with bars. Actually, there is no door at all. There are no privacy curtains, no rods or other things that people could use to hang themselves. There's a tiny window that looks out onto a brick wall, a narrow cot, and a small counter that holds a box of Kleenex. The bathroom is in the main area and does not lock. The nurses' station is surrounded by plexiglass and sits in the middle of the ward, affording the nurses a clear view of everything. We are monitored constantly, day and night. There is no privacy here.

My clothes and belongings were taken from me when I arrived, but the nurses have allowed me to hold on to my cellphone, which is a welcome distraction. Shortly, I am introduced to Ivan, the mental health worker on shift. Then, dinner arrives. The day has somehow passed quickly. To my surprise, I'm able to eat something, and a nurse tells me that I will initially need to eat small meals frequently.

A while later, a nurse brings in a woman who is extremely distraught. She informs him that sometimes she wants to be violent, and he asks if she wants to be violent now. Eventually, her unruliness causes the nurse to escort her to the little soundproof, padded room at the end of the hall. It is not soundproof enough to mask the screams.

I overhear a nurse mention that I may not be discharged tomorrow. This is concerning. I had never considered the possibility that I would be kept longer than overnight.

I decide to sleep in what I'm wearing; I feel too embarrassed to ask to change, or even to go to the bathroom. Mercifully, a nurse comes with a sedative so I can sleep amongst the chaos.

I'm hit by a wave of exhaustion, that comes from passing on the enormous burden I can no longer carry. Despite the constant commotion around me, I drift off to sleep. The decision has been made for me: I won't die today.

Day Two

It's 7:00 AM and already things are off to an eventful start. I'm awakened by Brandon—the talkative guy from the common room—pacing up and down the hall proclaiming, in very colourful language, that they shouldn't be keeping him here, and that he needs a cigarette. One room over, a woman is talking loudly on her cellphone. The stories she's telling to the person on the other end have little basis in reality.

The emergency psychiatric department is also home to substance use services, and there are people coming down from a variety of intoxicants. Brandon continues to yell, and people start yelling back at him: "Shut the fuck up, there are people trying to sleep!" I'm pretty sure a fight is about to break out, but Brandon surprises me by apologizing in what seems like a sincere manner, although he carries on with his tirade until a psych nurse intervenes. We don't hear anything for a while, and I vaguely wonder where he went. Perhaps to the padded room.

Another woman is disdainfully informing a nurse that she shouldn't be here because she isn't crazy. This really isn't a good way to make friends with other patients on a psych ward.

Shortly after, the nurse who is assigned to me for the day arrives with morning meds. She introduces herself as Morgan. I ask her if anything has arrived for me. Phone chargers are not permitted, so Jordan bought me a wireless charger and was to drop it off at the main entrance. Morgan says she doesn't think so, but promises to look into it.

Morgan tells me that Doctor Romano, the psychiatrist on duty, will talk to me shortly. She explains that because of COVID, I will use a phone at the nurses' station to talk to him. I should come when they page me so they can give me the phone. She shows me where to go and tells me to knock on the door of the nurses' station if I need anything at all. "It's just a temporary door, we have to get a new one," she says in a way that makes me think I really don't want to know what happened to the last one.

I return to my room and don't have to wait long before I'm called to the nurses' station and handed a phone. A nurse leads me into the same room I was in yesterday for a bit of privacy. The psychiatrist sounds like a jovial older man and he speaks very slowly. I suspect he is watching me on a monitor somewhere. Although I don't meet him in person, he somehow reminds me of a mall Santa Claus, or perhaps everyone's favourite uncle.

Doctor Romano asks all the same questions I was asked so many times the day before; my responses are almost becoming automatic. He seems concerned about my unintentional weight loss and understands my suicide plans without me having to go into too much detail. He asks if there is any family history of mental illness and at what age I began drinking and/or using recreational drugs.

After gathering a thorough history, he informs me that I will be transferred downstairs to the Inpatient Psychiatric Unit (IPU). The mystery of downstairs has been solved.

I return the phone to the nurses' station and head back to my room with little else to do. Morgan tells me she's called the main desk and the other psych wards and they can't find the charger that was dropped off for me. She says she'll go and check herself. I appreciate her kindness, taking time out of an incredibly busy shift to hunt down the missing charger. The nurses here are stretched thin, there is so much need.

I doze for a while. Morgan comes back, triumphantly holding up the wireless charger. I'm relieved. My phone, my lifeline to the world outside these walls, is almost dead. She also has a scale with her and says that Doctor Romano wants to get my weight. I stand on the scale and am surprised by the results: I weigh 30 pounds less than my lowest guess. I had no idea I'd let things get so out of control.

Morgan also tells me, rather regretfully, that they are still waiting for a bed to open downstairs. They do their best to transfer patients to the other psych wards as soon as they are stabilized, but, unfortunately, I'll be spending another night in psych emergency. I think of all the hospital beds reportedly left empty in fear of a surge in COVID-19 cases and have to laugh. The psych ward is still doing a brisk business; in fact, they tell me it's busier than ever.

That evening, there are a number of new people brought in. A woman is suffering a psychotic break. For everyone's safety, including her own, she is hauled off to the little padded room. A young father has just had his first panic attack and is convinced he's dying. My heart breaks for him; I know it likely won't be his last. They load him up on benzodiazepines to relax him and then send him home. He is bewildered and asks what he should do; he is told to make an appointment with his regular physician. He wants to know if he should ask the doctor for the same drugs they gave him here, and the nurse tells him the doctor likely won't prescribe them. Because of the potential for addiction, many doctors are cautious about prescribing benzodiazepines. It makes sense. Benzos have given me the only peace I've known in what feels like years; who wouldn't want that feeling to last?

This place is packed for tonight and, because of COVID, they can't put two people in a room together given the size of the space. People are lined up in cots down the hallway, and even in the meeting rooms.

Nurse Barb brings me hospital pyjamas, which are way too large. She comes back shortly with night meds and gives me a higher dose of sedative tonight. I think I'll need it. I sleep, but not particularly well, and I'm aware of the constant action on the ward. People drift in and out of my room, whether they are patients or nurses, I can't say.

Day Three

It's relatively calm and quiet this morning. I'm groggy from the sedative and dizzy from the side effects of the new medications the doctors have prescribed. Morgan comes with morning meds and checks my vitals.

Today, they will let me take a shower. I want to get the smell of this place off my skin. Being overly sensitive to smells, I am keenly aware of the antiseptic odour of the hospital, unwashed bodies, a faint undertone of human waste, and something else I can't quite put my finger on. If despair had a smell, I think it would smell like a hospital psychiatric emergency department.

Morgan unlocks the shower and holds out a clean shirt that sports the logo of a tourist destination on the island. Handing it to me, she says, "I've been waiting for someone really awesome to give this shirt to." If by "awesome" she means small, then I can see her point. It's the only garment they've given me in here that fits.

The shower is just a room, with a drain in the floor, that can easily be hosed down. There's a dispenser with an all-purpose body wash and shampoo, and nothing else. There is no curtain or place to hang clothes or towels. Morgan takes my street clothes to wash them for me.

Just the act of showering exhausts me, and I go back to my room and close my eyes. I overhear talk that there aren't any beds opening up downstairs, so no one will be transferred today. I'm surprisingly okay with that, as I've finally started to understand how this place works. The familiar chaos is somehow comforting.

Later, on my way to use the bathroom, a girl on one of the cots lining the hall calls out to me. She asks if I believe in God. I make a noncommittal noise. I'm not sure what the right answer is but I'm quite certain she could kick my ass if I got it wrong. This is not the time to get into disagreements, but I'm pretty sure there's no God in this place. There's no end to the depth of human suffering here.

I'm dozing in a drug-fuelled haze when Morgan comes to get me. She says I will be transferred today after all. This actually makes me nervous because I've come to know this ward and the people in it. Things make sense to me here, and I don't want to be uprooted and moved to a different ward. A girl in the hall overhears and tells me I'm lucky. She says they give you real cutlery down there instead of the disposable plastic stuff.

Morgan brings a wheelchair—it's hospital policy that patients are transferred between wards in this manner—and takes me through a maze of back hallways to a staff elevator. "We take patients through the back way so we're not parading you guys through the main part of the hospital," she explains. I wonder if it's so we won't try to make a run for it. I'm so dizzy and stoned I couldn't take five steps from the wheelchair; they don't have to worry about me running.

We arrive downstairs. This ward is much bigger and somewhat quieter. The floor and walls of the corridors are dark, with soft lighting. Morgan hands my belongings, including the clothes she has washed, to another nurse who inventories them, searching for any items that aren't allowed. She leaves, wishing me well, and I thank her profusely. I won't soon forget her kindness. I'm sad to see her go, leaving me in this strange place with nurses I don't know.

A care aide comes and wheels me to my room. Upstairs, nurses handle everything. Down here, psych nurses are the counsellors who also manage meds, and the aides bring meals and supervise patients when they're out of their rooms.

My new room is a regular hospital room. It's large enough to accommodate two beds, although there is only one. I stand from the wheelchair and sit down on the bed. "I think your nurse is Taylor, she should be in to see you soon," the aide says as she leaves. I wait alone on the bed, feeling lost in this strange place. A different aide comes in with dinner and asks if I've met my nurse yet. I say I haven't, and she goes in search of her.

After I eat, I scan the room for ways to die. Doing so has become so ingrained in me that it's almost automatic, but there's not much heart in it tonight. There is a cabinet with a few shelves in the corner and I put my things in it. In the IPU, they allow you to keep some of your belongings, mainly clothes. Upstairs in Psych Emergency, we had to ask anytime we wanted anything, and they would bring our bags, watching while we got what we needed. Patients are not allowed extra clothes or bags, because they might use them to strangle themselves. Things appear to be a little more relaxed here.

I listen to two Latina care aides gossip quietly in Spanish as they move clean laundry from a cart into the storage closet next to my room. I smile; the soft, familiar cadence instantly makes me feel more at home.

Eventually, Taylor, my night nurse, comes in. She asks me the standard questions every nurse asks when they come on shift. "On a scale from one to ten, how would you rate your mood?" "Any thoughts of suicide or self-harm?" "Any thoughts of hurting other people?" This last question makes me laugh a little; I'm always tempted to answer with, "Sure, do you want the list in alphabetical order?" Somehow, I don't think they'd find that funny in here.

She also asks me what goals I have for my time in hospital. I really have no idea. "Umm... develop better coping mechanisms to manage my depression and anxiety?" I say lamely.

She wants to know about my life on the outside, about my work, hobbies, family members and so on. She seems pleased that I'm a musician, and tells me there's a piano here if I want to play. I thank her, although I know I'll never take her up on it. The last thing I want is to draw attention to myself. I'm not here to meet people or make friends.

In a little while, Taylor comes back with night-time meds. The admitting doctor replaced the sleep med I came in on with one that has the option of a higher dose. So far, I haven't used it because they've been giving me benzodiazepines to sedate me at night. She says this ward is a little quieter, so she's going to give me the new sleep medication. If it doesn't work well, she'll give me the benzos.

This new medication is an epic failure. I sleep, but it's a sticky, agitated sleep in which I'm tormented by nightmares. The nurses, who do checks every fifteen minutes with their flashlights, enter my consciousness as hooded demons, illuminated by a backdrop of orange and yellow flames. I sweat profusely, and the line between sleep and wakefulness is blurry.

Day Four

I awake to a pounding in my head and the feeling that I haven't slept at all. It's early, about 7:00 AM. I answer a few texts, then try to get dressed, but there's a problem. This combination of meds is making me so dizzy I can barely stand. The vertigo is so bad that I vomit, and it takes me a good fifteen minutes to change into leggings and a shirt. Today I'm determined to have them see me somewhat put together in street clothes.

My day nurse has just come on shift. "Hey, I'm Emily, I'll be your nurse today," she says. "How are you doing this morning?"

"I don't feel so well, my stomach hurts," I mumble.

"That's a pretty common side effect of a couple of the medications you've started," she says sympathetically. "I'll talk to the doctors about getting you an antiemetic." Emily seems extremely caring and makes me feel at ease. I like her right away.

An announcement comes over the PA system telling all patients to return to their rooms as the breakfast trays have arrived. There is a dining room down the hall but, because of COVID, everyone must eat in their rooms. This is a relief, as shared meals would invite conversation I don't want.

My tray is delivered by a chatty, cheerful aide named Marisol. Now that I'm back sitting up in bed, the vertigo has diminished and, once again, I surprise myself by eating a bit.

Shortly after the breakfast trays have been taken away, Doctor Lewis, one of the psychiatrists, stops by on morning rounds. He is a very tall man in his late 40s. Muffled by a medical mask, he asks if we can chat for a bit. He pulls up the uncomfortable vinyl visitor's chair next to my bed and folds his lanky frame into it. "I've read your file," he says, "but why don't you tell me why you're here?" *God, they sure love this question.*

He accepts everything I say with the calmness and experience of someone who has heard it all a thousand times before. He surprises me by asking if I've heard the common refrain, "suicide is a permanent solution to a temporary problem," and I fight to suppress an eye roll. I wouldn't expect a doctor to say something so utterly cliche. Also, my problems aren't temporary, thank you very much.

"Do you have a plan?" he asks.

I tell him of the exit bag I'd planned to construct, and of my difficulties in procuring some of the necessary materials. "There's even a textbook that lays it all out," I add.

"I know," he says. "It's terrible."

I shrug. Terrible is not the word I'd use to describe it. Helpful and enlightening maybe. I also tell him of the final plan I'd settled on and how unhappy I was with it, how I felt like I had no other option, and was running out of time. I needed to die sooner rather than later.

"And what made you decide to come here first?"

"My aunt is an ER doctor," I say. "She said if I were one of her patients, this is where I'd need to be."

"I agree with her," he says bluntly.

"So," he asks, "you've told me the reasons you want to die, and how you plan to accomplish it, and this has obviously been a struggle for you for a long time. But what is it that's pushing you? Why now? What do you think is the common theme in all these reasons?"

I hesitate, thinking. "Control brought on by extreme perfectionism," I say finally. "I want to control everything and COVID came, and now I can't control anything, no matter what I do. I watch it all unfold, the closures and restrictions and the fear. I watch my plans unravel, the things I was really looking forward to, and I can't do a thing to change it. A lot of my loved ones live in other countries, and I have this fear that I'll never see them again. That maybe they'll forget me. I watch how people react to me, perfect strangers, and I can't control that either. I guess that's the thing that finally pushed me to the edge. There is way too much I can't control. It's all happened so fast, spinning further and further out of my grasp. I lost so much so quickly. And I guess that's why I want to die. It is the ultimate act of taking back control."

"But many of these things you feel you've lost and things you can't control, don't you think they'll come back after COVID?" he asks. "This will come to an end, you will see your loved ones again and be able to continue on with your plans."

"Maybe," I answer. "But that's not really the point. I don't know when that will be, and if I think about the 'when,' it's another thing I can't control. I have this fear of suddenly losing the people I love, this almost primal belief that I won't survive their abandonment. And many of those things that I wanted so badly, that were really coming together for me, I need them. They sustain me. Every day, I want to die," I explain. "But these things, when I knew when they were going to happen, I could count down to the happiness they were going to bring. I'd tell myself that I couldn't kill myself until after this really awesome thing had happened. Then I'd try and plan something else to look forward to so I could convince myself to keep living a little longer. My life is like a pond and the happy future things are like a bunch of lily pads and I'm the frog, leaping from one to another to be able to keep going. But then COVID came, and they all vanished. There's nothing sustaining me. I don't know if or when those things will come back."

"Hmm," he muses. "I'd call that living for the future. And the perfectionism you mention, does it stop you from doing things because you feel you'll never get them right? There's a fine line between perfectionism and what can be defined as a mental illness."

I tell him that's something that happens frequently. I am so worried that I'll make some sort of mistake out in public, especially something related to blindness, that some days I decide not to go out at all. The risk of someone seeing such a public display of imperfection often leaves me feeling like it's just not worth it to leave my house. Sometimes I forego playing music for long periods of time because I know I can't do it perfectly and, if it's not perfect, then what's the point of doing it?

He switches gears and asks me about my family history of mental illness. I tell him as much as I know, describing the severe anxiety, the paranoid behaviour and the bouts of depression I witnessed as a child.

"The mental illness you describe in your family has both a genetic and learned component," he says carefully.

I laugh, incredulous. Watching a loved one struggle with depression and anxiety every day shaped my childhood in many ways. Wouldn't I know if I had the same illness? Wouldn't I recognize the signs I was so intimately familiar with?

Doctor Lewis begins to ask questions about my actions and thoughts, to describe the lesser-known symptoms of the disease. And I know, he's describing me. Things slowly begin to click into place. Things that I thought were just my idiosyncrasies, things my friends and family would good-naturedly tease me about, like my complete inability to make decisions, my constant worry and fear, how I could always convince myself that the worst thing imaginable would happen at any moment.

They were actually symptoms of a debilitating mental illness.

He leaves me with these thoughts swirling around in my head and says we'll chat more tomorrow. How, in such a short hospital stay, were they able to tell me things so many doctors and psychotherapists had previously missed? Had a medical professional ever suspected but never told me? Did they not ask the right questions, or did I not give the right answers? Didn't my loved ones see it? More importantly, how the hell did I miss the signs in myself? I want to reject it all as stupid psychobabble from a doctor who doesn't even know me, but I can't.

I wonder if the depression and anxiety, and the unintentional weight loss are, in part, the symptoms and not the cause. Is there something bigger at play here? My heart aches for all the lost years. If we had only known earlier, maybe I wouldn't have had to struggle for so long. I am angry. If life had turned out how it was supposed to, I should have been in the therapist's chair, and some other person would be in this bed. But I latch on, with relief, to the knowledge that there is a genetic component to this disease. Maybe I will eventually stop seeing this situation as all my fault.

I lie back in bed and listen to the hospital sounds: the PA announcements paging various patients and medical staff to the nurses' station; the squeak of rubber-soled shoes on the tile floor; the rattle of hospital carts; a nurse and patient walking by.

"I just can't understand why you'd set that on fire," the nurse admonishes a patient. I can't hear the patient's reply; I probably don't want to.

A short time later, Marisol comes in and asks if I want to sit in the solarium. I don't. But I realize I'm probably expected to leave my room at some point, so I agree.

The solarium is a small, warm room filled with plants and sunlight. Banks of chairs line two of the walls. I've brought my headphones even though I'm not listening to any music; it's an attempt to avoid conversation with other patients. It doesn't work.

"Hey, you're new," says another patient, plopping down in a chair to my right. "You have a bracelet, where are you from?"

I know he must be referring to my hospital bracelet, but I can't figure out how these two things are related. "Uh, the island?" It comes out sounding more like a question than an answer—I am intentionally vague.

"No," he says as if speaking to a dim child. "What ward were you sent from? PES? PICU?"

I don't yet know all of the acronyms used by the more initiated, so I tell him I came from upstairs.

"Your bracelet means you'll get discharged," he explains.

Well, I sure as hell hope so.

He has helped me understand that, between patients, the presence of a hospital bracelet indicates a patient has a good chance of getting out of this place, and won't necessarily simply be transferred to another ward or facility. Whether this assumption is based in reality, I don't know.

"I'm being discharged too," he continues.

"When?" I ask to be polite.

"Maybe in a week or something," he says absently. "I'm excited to get my things back, I have half a bottle of vodka in lockup at the nurses' station." I realize he must have been brought in with the alcohol in his possession. "But it's not so bad in here if people bring you things," he goes on. "Yesterday my wife dropped me off a bowl of chili from Wendy's."

Because there are no visitors allowed due to COVID, any items brought for patients must be dropped off at the hospital's main entrance where they stay until someone has time to transport them to the correct ward. The chili must have been ice cold by the time it got to him.

"You know, I'm an engineer," he tells me. "I actually worked on this hospital." My bullshit meter has certainly improved since I've had to listen to the stories of delusional patients, but I actually believe him. It makes me sad. I hope he'll get better. So many people here are stuck in a never-ending loop, being bounced between institutions, sent back into the community, ending up in rehab or jail, returning to the psych ward and on and on it goes.

The PA announcement that lunch has arrived mercifully cuts our conversation short, and I half run back to the safety of my room.

After lunch, Marisol asks if I want to go back out to the solarium. I agree, because she's really nice, and also because I don't know how to say no. Massive rain clouds have rolled in, and I sit in the solarium listening to the steady, soothing thrum of rain against the glass roof.

Soon, Emily comes to find me. We are alone in the solarium, and she asks if we can sit here and chat. She has some papers in her hand.

"I've been reading your file," she tells me. "That's some really tough stuff, and for a long time," she says gently. "Because of your current struggles and your history, the doctors have decided it's best to continue with your treatment here in the hospital, as an involuntary patient under the BC Mental Health Act. Which means that, like in the past few days, you won't be free to leave."

She begins to read from the papers in her hand. She is reading me my rights while I'm detained under the act, much like a person who gets arrested is mirandized. I've overheard this happen to other patients, and many argue. I don't, I understand why. The doctors are just doing their job. Ethically, they need to try to keep me alive. That's what doctors do, after all.

Doctor Lewis has completed my second certificate, which means I can now be held here for a period of up to one month.

Emily has me sign the document, which strikes me as a bit odd. It's not like I can disagree. I suppose it's just to confirm that I understand my rights as she's read them to me.

"I'll be your nurse for the next four days," she tells me. I'm comforted by this—she is around my age and sympathetic without being condescending. Clearly dedicated to the well-being of the patients in her care, she has quickly become my favourite nurse on the ward. Perhaps she is someone I could have been friends with, had we met under different circumstances.

Emily gives me a tour of the ward. She points out the nurses' station, the showers (locked of course), a laundry machine where patients can wash their own clothes, the activity room, and the dining room where the piano sits.

We end the tour back in my room. I sink down onto the raised hospital bed and she sits in the chair Doctor Lewis had used earlier. The psych nurses are active participants in patient treatment plans and reinforce what we work on in our sessions with the psychiatrists. Instead of long therapy sessions, we have shorter, almost impromptu, sessions with our nurse throughout the day and evening.

Emily asks if I've done any cognitive behavioural therapy before. Having taken psychology courses in university, I am familiar with the concept; if only I were better at putting it into practice. The general idea of CBT is to identify negative or inaccurate thinking and practice techniques for re-shaping that thinking. People are encouraged to ask themselves hard questions about whether their thinking is accurate, or if it is based on an inaccurate perception of reality. CBT is based on the belief that reshaping negative thinking can reshape our perception of ourselves to be more positive, as well as help with resilience and coping with difficult situations. In few words, "Change your thinking, change your life."

We start with something simple: my feelings around spending more time in the common areas. We examine the narrative I tell myself: "Everyone is staring and judging; I'll do something embarrassing; nobody will like me," to a more accurate assessment of the situation, "People are generally good and see the positive qualities in others; I'm a valuable person with as much right as anyone to be there."

"Can you name some positive qualities you see in yourself?" Emily asks.

This is really hard. If she'd asked me for negative ones, I could have gone on all day.

"Umm, I'm an okay musician," I say halfheartedly.

"Good, that's a start," she says. "You only just got here, we'll keep working on it."

She tells me about the daily group wellness sessions that are offered. They are an hour long and start with group therapy, finishing with a wellness activity such as meditation or yoga. She asks if she can put me on the list for tomorrow's session. I've always figured group therapy would be terrifying and completely useless, but nothing about this experience has been easy. Hell, I'm here anyways, I may as well put in a bit of effort.

I agree and she seems pleased. She gets up and tells me she'll check in with me again soon.

Out in the hall, I hear the shrill voice of Karen, AKA the "I'm not crazy" lady from that eventful first morning in the emergency psych ward. She has just been transferred to the ward and is already complaining about the hospital blankets and the location of her room. I guess she missed the memo about this not being a five-star resort—more like the Hotel California.

Emily comes back a while later with a bag of clothes and snacks I'd asked Jordan to drop off. I never expected to be here this long, so didn't pack enough, and the hospital garb is hideous. The Pringles and Aero bars are a welcome treat from the monotony of bland hospital food. She empties the bag in front of me and sorts through all the clothes inside to make sure there's nothing I can't have; I feel a little embarrassed that she is seeing my underwear.

"Anything you need before I go off shift?" she asks.

"I've been wondering, what are the acronyms for the different wards here? What does PES mean?"

"Right now, you're in the IPU, inpatient psychiatric unit," she explains. "When you were first admitted, you were in PES, psychiatric emergency services. There's another ward, the PICU, psychiatric intensive care unit, where extremely violent or unpredictable patients are treated."

Mystery solved.

Dinner comes soon after, and Taylor comes to chat. She asks how my day went, although I'm sure she already knows. Nurses and doctors have meetings when they come on shift, during which they discuss the progress and treatment plans of the patients in their care, as well as read progress notes written by the nurse on the previous shift.

We continue with the CBT I had been working on earlier in the day with Emily. None of this stuff is new to me, but repetition is the name of the game. While I'm here, I will receive intensive therapy, constant reminders to form healthier ways of thinking, and support to find better coping strategies.

I spend the late evening texting with friends and family, and after Taylor comes with night-time meds, I fully intend to sleep. I've been going to bed early every night so far, aided by the meds, and the fact that there's not much else to do in here.

They decide not to give me the sleep medication that caused me such problems the night before, and I forego the stronger sedatives for now. Taylor reminds me they're there if I need them.

I listen to music and try to fall asleep, but this night is different. I am restless, hyper aware and mildly euphoric. I know this is caused by the rapid changes and increases in medications. When physicians or mental health professionals talk about the risk of antidepressants leading to suicide, they often refer to this kind of rapid increase in energy. Because severe depression typically leaves a person completely exhausted, a sudden increase in energy can give a suicidal patient the energy needed to enact their plan to die.

I try to stay in bed, but I'd much rather be running laps than sleeping. My thoughts are racing from one place to another. I feel like superwoman. If I could jump off a roof right now, I'm almost sure I could fly. It's a strange state to be in, and yet when Taylor looks in during her rounds, I pretend to be asleep so she won't give me a sedative.

Just when I think maybe I can sleep for a bit, I hear the medivac helicopter arrive. They are presumably transporting a critically ill or injured patient from a smaller community to a larger hospital for treatment. Its landing is so loud that the ground shakes, the windows rattle, and I have the disconcerting feeling that it'll come right through the building.

Shortly after, an announcement comes over the PA system. "Code blue! I repeat, code blue!"

The bed number of the patient is given, somewhere in the ER. I've watched enough medical dramas on TV to know that code blue is the hospital code for a patient in respiratory or cardiac arrest, requiring immediate emergency intervention.

And that's when it hits me.

I've never taken much stock in epiphanies, believing that changes in thinking come about gradually. But several thoughts slam into my consciousness at once, hard enough to take my breath away. I realize that somewhere out there, someone's loved ones are having one of the scariest nights they will ever know. The unknown stranger in the bed upstairs is someone's mother or father, brother or sister, grandparent, child or best friend. On the floor above where I lie right now, someone is fighting for their life, while I still want so desperately to end mine. And I wonder, if given the choice, would they trade their life for mine?

My heart swells with compassion for this person and for everyone who loves them. How could I feel so much empathy for their loved ones, while knowing the action I want to take will devastate my own.

My life plays before me on a silent movie reel, my mind scanning back through the years. I think of the things I accomplished, and the many others I had planned and not yet done. Just maybe, there's some small bit of good left for me to do in this world before I leave it.

As I lie in a hospital bed, ten minutes and a world away from home, I suddenly realize I must fight to find a way forward. I make a promise to myself. I will share my story so that, maybe someday, someone won't have their own similar story to tell. I will speak this all-too-common truth for so many people who no longer can, the ones who have been lost to this terrible, heartbreaking disease. I feel a desperate need for my story to be more than just a tragedy. Perhaps it can offer a glimmer of hope or comfort to someone else. If my story can reach even one person, then all of this won't be in vain. I haven't been able to choose to stay for myself, or even for my loved ones. But for some reason, the thought of some future nameless, faceless stranger going through all this pain is too much to bear.

Tonight, I choose life.

Day Five

It's just getting light out when Taylor comes in to find me sitting up in bed. My legs jiggle up and down restlessly and my hands fidget in my lap. She asks me how my night was.

"It was okay, I didn't sleep because the helicopter came and then there was the code blue and I just couldn't relax," I tell her. I'm aware that I'm speaking way too fast.

I ask if I can take a shower. She tells me they don't open until later in the morning, presumably when more staff are available to monitor them. Now that Taylor knows I'm awake, I get up and pace the room, no longer able to stay in bed. I am dimly aware that at some point I'm going to come down off this high, hard. I wonder just how epic that crash will be.

Breakfast arrives early. I was hoping to shower before eating, so I don't miss Doctor Lewis on his rounds, but it'll have to wait.

Emily pops her head in as I'm finishing a bowl of tasteless oatmeal. "I heard you had quite the night," she says.

I ask if she thinks I have time to shower before the doctors do their rounds. "Yeah," she answers, "the docs usually don't start until later, around nine-thirty or so."

She adopts a fake, upper class British accent and intones, "Yes, the doctors are in."

Laughing, I stand and follow her down the hall. She ducks behind the nurses' station to grab me some shampoo and conditioner and tells me to meet her at the showers.

As I continue down the corridor, a girl calls out to me, "Hey, you're doing awesome! Keep it up." I smile as I pass her. I can't detect even the slightest hint of condescension in her tone.

Emily arrives moments later, apologizing that she can only find men's shampoo. A care aide stationed outside the shower door asks if I want her to help wash me. I quickly decline, slightly mortified. As with the shower in PES, there is nowhere to hang clothes or towels. I stand under the warm spray, which irritatingly turns itself off every thirty seconds. The shampoo Emily brought me smells like Axe body spray. I'm going to smell like the goddamn jock hallway in my high school before a football match. I'm still dizzy and nauseated from the meds, so the smell of the shampoo sends a wave of nausea over me. I lean against the wall of the shower and try to breathe through it.

By the time I get back to my room, I'm tired from the effort and the lack of sleep. I dress in jeans and a T-shirt and force myself to make my way to the common room, positioning myself in the chair nearest the door so I can make a hasty retreat if anything goes awry. Truthfully, I know that even if it does, the most likely outcome is that

I'll stay frozen to this spot. Every nerve ending in my body is on high alert for the slightest perceived danger. This isn't because I'm in the psych ward and scared of the other patients, it's simply my body's response to being in an unknown situation with unknown people. This strong, fearful fight-or-flight response is my daily reality, and I realize how exhausting it has been.

The TV is on, and for the first time since I've been here, I catch a bit of the news. COVID numbers continue to climb; there are protests and riots happening everywhere. It strikes me that being in here is like being in a bubble. Ironically, I've heard little about COVID since I arrived at the hospital.

It's quiet in here, early in the day. Two girls sit at a table chatting; one is giving life advice to the other. The girl playing therapist is going home today. She talks of her newfound mental stability with the fervour of a religious zealot. I wonder if I'll sound like that when I get out of here. She gives her friend a painting she's made to remember her by, and they are both crying.

A boy who sounds like he's not much more than a teenager speaks quietly on his cellphone. "I'm sorry, I can't," he says to the person on the other end. "I'm in the hospital quarantining because of COVID." He is under a quarantine of sorts I suppose, but COVID has nothing to do with it. He seems desperately sad. I hope he has someone on the outside supporting him, someone he can be truthful with.

A few minutes pass and Brandon walks into the common room—I guess he got transferred here from PES too—and begins negotiating with another patient. It seems Brandon has a friend or family member who is bringing him things, and he is making a list of other patients' requests for chocolate bars, chips, candy, gum, and various other treats. Brandon seems to have quite the entrepreneurial streak. He also seems a lot more relaxed in here than he was in PES.

I listen idly to the negotiations until Doctor Lewis pokes his head in, looking for me. He asks if I can take him back to my room. I wonder if this is some sort of test to see if I've learned my way around yet.

We assume the same positions as yesterday: him in the visitor's chair and me sitting up in the bed. "How are you feeling today? Any thoughts of suicide?" he asks.

"Yeah, but I wouldn't actually try anything in the hospital. I mean, I'm a numbers and probability girl," I say with a bit of a laugh. "What are the chances I'd actually be successful in here? And I'm a perfectionist. I'm not going to do something if I think it's likely to fail. The temptation just doesn't exist right now."

"Makes sense," he responds. There is a brief silence before he says, "You know, I'm still having a hard time putting together what you mean about suicide being the ultimate act of control. You're gonna have to spell it out for me a bit more clearly."

I know the promise I made to myself last night and all, but I'm instantly annoyed. He knows exactly what I mean, and we both know it. By spelling it out, he's hoping I'll stumble upon the flaws in my own thinking.

"How isn't it? The ultimate act of control I mean. What gives someone more control than controlling exactly how and when they'll die?"

"But in dying, you're giving up control," he says. "Isn't it kind of the opposite? Things are so out of control that you kill yourself?"

"I guess so, but who cares about what comes after?" I ask. "I won't feel the need to control anything because I won't be here."

"But I still don't really see how dying means you're in control," he says.

"It's a bit ironic," I say, half to myself. "Loss of control is the thing I'm most afraid of, and yet somehow I've ended up here, where I pretty much have no control over anything at all."

"True," he says. "So why do you think you made the choice to come here?"

"I don't know," I say truthfully. "I guess I just wanted to know I'd tried everything."

He changes direction. "Want to talk about how your night was?" I tell him about the code blue and how anxious it made me feel, then how stupid I felt after for being upset over something that didn't involve me—a situation in which I had no control over the outcome.

"So, you beat yourself up about it," he says. "And there's empathy in hearing those things and feeling for another person, but again we come back to your feeling of helplessness to control things that happen that are out of your hands. What do you think you could tell yourself to let go of those repetitive, negative thoughts in a similar situation?"

I pick at a loose thread on my jeans as I ponder this for a minute. "I guess that it's all right to feel for that person and their family, but there are good people who are dealing with the situation. That it's out of my control, and that's okay. I need to relax, and trust that there is someone managing the situation."

"Did you know researchers found that an emotion lasts only seven minutes?" he asks. I'm surprised by this. "Emotions are very short-lived, unless we keep circling back to them. So, any pain you're feeling, any anxiety, know that those emotions will pass in a short amount of time. They don't need to continue indefinitely."

I find this oddly comforting. "You know, when I'm happy, I'm already sad, thinking of how it will end and I'll need to survive until the next good thing comes along."

"You're a lily pad jumper," he says, referring to my comments from the previous day. I'm impressed, he doesn't record our sessions and he isn't taking any notes. "Living in the moment is important for well-being, and it takes practice. For example, right now, we're sitting here having a nice conversation, and you know that it'll come to an end. You could anticipate that ending, or you could practice living in this moment, enjoying it for the time it lasts."

144

I find it a bit amusing that he finds our psych-ward conversation about death "enjoyable," but then I realize it kind of is for me too. Although it's easier said than done, he has a point. Why can't I allow myself to fully feel the joy of a precious moment, as strongly as I will inevitably feel the pain of it being over when that time comes?

"Have you discussed the theory of radical acceptance in therapy before?" he asks.

I'm familiar with it, Chris and I have talked about it in our sessions many times. "Yeah, it's pretty much as it sounds, right? We accept the pain, the emotions, and the situation we are in at any given time; we practice a complete acceptance of reality as it is and not how we wish it to be. We accept that we are exactly where we need to be in that precise moment."

"Good," he says, after I relay my understanding of it to him. "Then maybe part of your healing can be accepting your reality. As an example, your blindness. You fight others' perceptions of it, but maybe your acceptance means that you are in a place or a moment to show someone else what it is to overcome adversity."

I am instantly frustrated. "But who gets to decide that's my purpose?" I ask, when what I really want to say is *but I never asked to be anyone's fucking inspiration.*

"I suppose that depends on what you believe," he muses.

"But what if my inner five-year-old is throwing a tantrum and screaming 'No! I don't want to!'"

"Well," he says, "practicing acceptance doesn't mean you have to like something or that it's okay, or that you have to excuse it. It's simply acknowledging what is happening. Actually, I'm glad you brought that up. Are you familiar with the family systems theory?"

"Not really," I tell him.

"Basically," he explains, "each family member affects every other family member. Look it up on the weekend and do some reading about it.

"That reminds me," he says, "do you have an iPad or anything with screen-reading software so you're able to communicate with your partner and others who are supporting you?"

I tell him I do, patting my iPhone beside me on the bed. It surprises me that he knows what a screen reader is, let alone that he thinks to ask me about it.

"Good, I just wanted to make sure you have everything you need and don't need us to do anything to facilitate that. Also, before I go, I wanted to ask you about your weight. What is your perception of yourself? Physically I mean."

"I don't know, I don't really have anything to compare it with."

"What do you think about your current weight and how it makes you look?"

"It's fine, I guess. I mean, I suppose I see it as a benefit, but I didn't stop eating because of that."

"Hmm," he muses. "So, imagine you were, say... ninety pounds. How would you feel about that?"

"Fine, I guess." I shrug.

"How about ninety-five? A hundred?"

"Still fine."

He continues in five-pound increments until I stop him.

"Okay," he says neutrally.

"Oh, and one last thing," he adds. "Would you like me to get the results of your genetic testing so we can help you process them while you're here in the hospital?"

In the chaos of everything, I had almost forgotten that I would have been going to Vancouver in exactly a week to find out whether or not I'm a candidate for gene therapy to restore my vision. I say that I would, but that I'm not sure if COVID will have changed the timing, or even if the results will come in at all.

"Well," he says, "I'll talk to the specialist, doc to doc, and I'll see what I can find out."

I thank him and he leaves to continue his rounds. I lie back on the bed, my head swimming. I feel like we've just had an hour-long debate on my right to die, and he's too smart for me. I'd say he definitely won this time. It feels like I've endured the psychological equivalent of going ten rounds with Mike Tyson.

Emily stops by a little later. "How'd it go with Doctor Lewis?"

"Fine," I say. "We talked about the theory of radical acceptance."

"Oh, perfect, DBT, I was actually going to ask you if we could work on that a bit this afternoon."

"DBT?" I ask. I know it's a specific type of CBT, but I haven't explored it in detail.

"The theory of radical acceptance is part of dialectical behaviour therapy," she explains. "DBT focuses on learning to accept what is out of our control while teaching healthy coping skills to replace unhealthy, negative and/or dangerous behaviours. These strategies seem like polar opposites, which is where the name 'dialectical'—the existence of opposites—comes from." She places a blood pressure cuff around my arm and inflates it as she speaks.

"How are you feeling right now?" she asks. "Any thoughts of suicide?"

I repeat what I told Doctor Lewis, that I wouldn't be inclined to try anything here, because my chances of success would be slim.

"If you had something right here beside you in this moment that you could use, do you think you would?"

"Yeah," I say without hesitation. I knew I didn't believe in epiphanies.

"Thank you for being honest, that's important to recovery," she says. I have nothing left to lose, what would be the point in lying?

"Can you tell me one thing you did so far today that you're proud of?" she asks.

I think for a minute. "Uh, I left my room and took a shower," I say, laughing a little.

"That's totally legitimate. You have to be proud of yourself for every one of the steps you take. Sometimes

148

even small tasks can seem momentous with depression. Do you have any goals for yourself today?"

"Hmm," I hesitate. "Talk to two people I don't know."

"That's a great goal to work toward," she says with enthusiasm.

"So, how are you feeling about group wellness today? Want to give it a try?" she asks as she gathers up her nursing equipment and prepares to leave. I agree, and she says she'll let the facilitator know, and that she'll likely come and introduce herself before the session.

"Oh," she says, turning in the doorway and stepping back into the room, "the doc is a bit concerned about your weight. He'd like you to drink an Ensure® with breakfast and dinner to up your calorie intake and help correct some nutritional deficiencies he suspects, as well as take some vitamins in the morning. Does that all sound okay to you?"

I'm not sure how I feel about being made to drink Ensure®, which I will always associate with visiting my great grandmother in a nursing home when I was a kid, but I tell her it's fine.

"He's ordered some blood tests to get a clearer picture of nutritional deficiencies, so someone will come early tomorrow morning from the lab to draw blood. They'll also come later today to do an ECG. Doctor Lewis just wants to make sure everything is okay with your heart. One of your new medications can

149

occasionally cause heart problems, so we just want to check that everything is good."

The lunch trays come, but I'm preoccupied with thoughts of the upcoming group therapy session and I can't eat much.

The group facilitator, Christina, stops by as the aides are clearing the lunch trays. She introduces herself, says she's glad to have me join group, and asks if there's anything I need from her. I tell her I'm fine, and she says she'll see me shortly.

A nurse stops by with a gift bag in his hand. Today is apparently International Donut Day, as evidenced by a post I was tagged in by Chelsea on Facebook. My mom, who was passing through my city and happened to see said Facebook post, has dropped off a treat from my favourite donut shop. I wish I had the appetite for them, but it feels like all I do in here is eat.

I give my mom a brief call to thank her; she sounds relieved to hear from me and says I sound a lot better. It's probably the lingering high from last night. It has been hard to talk to my family over the past months, I feel like I'll be letting them down, but I've been too exhausted to make the effort to act as if everything is okay, or to answer a barrage of unwanted questions.

I constantly check the clock on my phone, counting down the minutes until I need to go to group. When the time comes, I take a deep breath, gather my resolve and head out the door and down the hall to the room where Christina told me the group would be meeting.

I arrive two minutes early. So far, there is only one other girl sitting in the circle of chairs set up in the middle of the room. I take the chair nearest the door, just in case, and, remembering the goal I'd set with Emily, I turn to her. "Hey," I say, "have you done this before?"

"Yeah," she mutters as if I'm stupid. *Alrighty then, so much for that.* She wanders out the door, and another girl sits down. I recognize her. She's Janelle, the girl from the common room that Brandon was talking to my first day in PES.

"Hey," I say.

"Hey, it's really cold in here, isn't it?" she says, rubbing her arms.

I can't put my finger on exactly what it is, but I see something in her I recognize in myself, and feel an instant kinship with her. I think of us as comrades in this strange place. I realize I'm actually sweating.

Eventually, our small group has assembled and Christina closes the door. She asks us to go around the circle and state our names, as well as how we're feeling today. I've hated this particular icebreaker in any group I've ever been a part of.

When my turn comes, I say my name and that I'm feeling anxious. I'm able to say it easily, and I realize how refreshing it is to not have to pretend to be okay in here. I don't need to sit in the common room and pretend I have no fear, or to sit here in this circle and tell everyone I'm great as I try to stop my hands from shaking. None of us are okay. If we were, we wouldn't be here.

"So, today we had a request to talk about boundaries," Christina says.

"Great," one girl says. "Boundaries will be useful when... if… I'm able to get out of here someday."

I wonder if she has a bracelet. My vision isn't good enough to see such a minute detail.

Patients in the group seem a little awkward. Everyone talks over one another, and many of their ramblings are difficult to understand. One girl, Erin, is complaining about another patient she doesn't like, and Christina tries to redirect her, reminding her not to use the names of other patients who aren't in group. "But he's such a jerk to me!" she exclaims exasperatedly. "He said a painting I made the other day was awful!"

"A situation like that could be a good opportunity to practice boundaries," Christina says. "What are some approaches we can take to let someone know a comment they've made or something they've done has hurt us or made us feel uncomfortable?"

"I don't know, that guy's just a jerk," Erin sulks. "I just told him not to be so rude. How would he like it if I insulted something he worked really hard on?"

Another girl begins agitatedly muttering to herself. I can't understand her words, but I'm pretty sure whatever she's saying has nothing to do with boundaries. I realize that Janelle and I are the only non-confused patients in attendance. Perhaps the patients who have been here longer know something we don't. We are also the only ones who don't speak. Things are rather tangential and don't tend to stay on topic, but mainly I'm just bored and thinking I'm not getting much out of this.

Then Paul, the heavyset, middle-aged man slumped in the chair directly to my left, cuts through my boredom, completely shattering the relative calm I had begun to feel. "The doctors in here are such thugs. Like Doctor Lewis, he just lets guys go who aren't supposed to get out and makes the rest of us stay in here. The psychiatrists think they're real gangsters or something. Like they're real hot shit." He is alluding to what I already suspected: there are people in here because they aren't mentally sound enough to be in jail.

Christina asks him to watch his language and tries to steer the topic back to boundaries, but Paul interrupts her. "You know, speaking of boundaries, I feel like you're being really controlling, you're monopolizing the conversation and acting like you're better than us." The older woman sitting across from me pipes up, agreeing with Paul.

Isn't the point of a group facilitator to kind of, like, facilitate the group?

"Okay," says Christina, "thank you for letting me know that you're feeling that way—"

"You know, it's like I have no rights," Paul continues, deadly serious. "Like all these people in this country can have their freedom of religion and expression and all that shit, they get to do what they want, but if my religion is molesting children, why don't I have the freedom to do that? Canada and the US are so strict, violating my rights. They should loosen up."

My blood runs cold. There is stunned silence. Every part of me wants to flee, but I'm glued to my seat. All of a sudden, I am not in this room with these people, but in a very different place, at a very different time. Whether it's the tone of his voice or the words he speaks, I do not know, but things from so long ago come rushing back to me with perfect clarity. It's not Paul's voice I hear in my head now, but a voice I haven't heard in so many years. For a moment, I am a scared child once more.

Janelle stands up abruptly, mumbling something about needing a drink of water. Christina calmly tries to redirect the conversation. Somehow, the group continues, although I am no longer aware of what is being said. Mercifully, the sharing portion eventually ends, and Christina says we are going to practice a guided meditation.

"I'm leaving, I hate meditation," says Paul. The lady across from me once again agrees with him, and they stand together and make their way to the door.

I try to find some comfort in the meditation, but I can't practice deep breathing when I'm struggling to breathe at all. A distraught woman runs past in the hall. "I am not an animal!" she screams, over and over again. Her hysteria only adds to my mounting distress.

As soon as Christina turns on the lights and announces the end of the session, I bolt from my chair. I barely make it back to the safety of my room before I collapse. Managing to pull myself onto the bed, I curl into a tight ball. In my mind, I am screaming.

One of the mental health workers pops his head around the door and asks if I want a snack. "No!" I say, more harshly than I had intended. I just need him to leave.

I lie in the darkened hospital room and am overcome by a grief more profound than any I have ever known. Suddenly, I'm crying for it all: the entirety of the mess that has led me to this moment. How did I fuck everything up so badly? How did I end up here? I had wanted so much more for my life than this.

I cry for the pain of the past and the fear of the future. My heart aches so much I fear it will literally shatter in my chest. I am crying so hard I can no longer breathe. And then, Christina walks in and sees me lying crumpled on the bed. I barely have the wherewithal to feel embarrassed that a stranger is seeing me in this state.

"Hey, I just wanted to check on you to see how you found... oh, what's wrong? Was it group?"

"I don't know," I somehow manage to choke out. "I guess I'm homesick." I cannot find words to tell her the whole truth. She says that's understandable and tries to distract me, asking me about my hobbies and my life on the outside. It doesn't work, and she leaves to get Emily.

There are more patients yelling now. That one distressed woman who was screaming during meditation set off the others. I just want it to stop. I have never felt more out of control in my life. I am locked in here with

155

people like Paul who believe such sick things, and I have no way of escape.

Emily walks in. "Hey, are you okay?" she asks. All I can do is lie there, my body wracked with silent sobs. Eventually, I am able to tell her what was said in group. She seems appalled. "I'm so sorry. I would be really upset hearing that too."

"I never said goodbye," I sob. "I just never expected this would happen."

"What do you mean?"

"The day I was admitted. I never thought they'd keep me. I never said goodbye and now I'm in here and I have no idea when I'll get to go home." Even in this state, the irony is not lost on me. How can I be missing a home and people that I intended to leave anyway?

Emily makes a sympathetic noise but says nothing. She just sits next to the bed and waits until I am able to speak. "I hadn't cried since I got here," I say finally. "Not even in PES."

Emily is surprised. "Really? Then it was your time," she says gently. "This place is made of tears."

She helps me drink from a cup of water on the table next to my bed. "Please," she asks, "will you let me give you something?" She is referring to a sedative. It strikes me then that if someone were in the hospital in acute physical pain, they would not be left to suffer. They would be given something to take the pain away. Why are we programmed to view emotional pain so differently?

I nod my reply and she leaves.

A moment later, she comes back with the drugs. "I'll give you this dose for now, and I can give you another in forty-five minutes if you need it. I don't want to give you too much and have it interfere with your ECG. They should be here from the lab really soon.

"You know, this is okay. This is good. You've dropped that mask we've all been seeing since you got here, the girl who has it all together and can do everything. You were brave to go to group today. I hope you realize how strong you are, truly. You've been fighting this so hard for such a long time."

This makes me cry harder. As I lie here, shattered and broken in a hospital bed, I feel anything but strong.

Emily steps out of the room for a minute and I get the terrible idea that I should respond to some messages as a way to distract myself while I wait for the sedative to take effect. I answer an audio message from a friend. I'm crying so hard the message is almost unintelligible. Only a few phrases are clear, "I don't belong here, I want to go home. I have no idea when they'll let me go home."

Things start to become hazy. Dinner arrives but I don't eat. A woman comes from the lab to do my electrocardiogram. She attaches the probes to my body with practiced efficiency and barely speaks. I feel like she doesn't want to be here either. It is done in a matter of minutes, and Emily comes to give me another dose of sedative.

I am swimming down, down, down. My very last thought is: *This isn't how my life was supposed to go.* Then there's only sweet, painless nothingness.

Day Six

I wake up slowly. It must be late. My untouched breakfast tray sits on the rolling table next to my bed. I grab my phone to check the time and see a series of concerned texts. The events of the previous day come rushing back. I have no memory of anything after I was given the sedative at around 5:30 PM, although I suppose they must have wakened me enough so I could swallow my night-time meds.

I vaguely recall the presence of a soft-spoken young lab tech sitting beside my bed in the early morning hours. I would have thought I dreamt it, were it not for the cotton ball taped to my inner elbow where they'd drawn blood.

There's a tap on the door, and a man I don't know pushes it open. "Hey, I'm Brett, your nurse for today." He's so young and appears tentative and awkward. I have the impression he drew the weekend shift but doesn't normally work on this ward. He seems almost scared of me. I wonder why, I'm one of the compliant ones. There are patients in here who would eat him alive if they sensed his unease. Then I realize what my progress report from yesterday must look like.

He asks me the standard questions, which are now so familiar I could answer them in my sleep, which I

159

probably did last night. His awkwardness makes me awkward; he hands me a small cup of pills and beats a hasty retreat, saying he'll check in later. He seems only too glad to leave.

Things are quiet this morning. I wish Emily would come, then I remember she said she would be working night shift today. The psychiatrists don't do general rounds on weekends. I lie back and drift, on the cusp between sleep and wakefulness. I am still so very tired. A storm is raging outside; rain pours down in torrents, and thunder crashes loudly enough to be heard over the din of the hospital.

Lunch is delivered by a pleasantly plump, extremely gregarious older care aide who appears to be the "mother" of the ward. I still feel nauseated, I haven't even been able to touch my donuts from yesterday, a tragedy in my mind.

And then, not long after the lunch trays are taken away, an aide discovers a patient face down in the toilet in his room.

At first glance, the aide thinks he is being sick and offers to get him a container to throw up into. She draws nearer and gets a clear look. "Oh! No, no…" She sounds ill herself now.

Nurses hurry in to help. They get the patient onto his bed, and a doctor arrives. He will be okay. He is given more meds, and all is quiet.

My heart is pounding. Although I don't fully understand how he did it, with sick horror I relive the past few moments. I can see him there in my mind's eye lying face down in filth. And I realize that, in all the ways I had thought of to die, this one had never crossed my mind. I couldn't imagine being so desperate that they would find my body afterwards, my head in the toilet like a dog.

I wonder if the outcome would have been different if this had happened earlier in the day, during morning shift change when there is the least supervision and the staff are most distracted. I realized soon after I arrived, in the unlikely event that I got desperate enough to attempt suicide in here, morning would be the best time to try.

I can't shake the images from my head, and waves of nausea roll through me. I fight to control my breathing. I am going to have a panic attack.

While the patient is still asleep, maintenance arrives to empty the toilet and turn off the water. The whole thing is handled with such efficiency that I'm confident he is not the first to have done this. I'm sure he won't be the last.

For some reason, late afternoons are when many patients become restless and agitated, and this holds true for today. Brandon is talking loudly on the phone at the nurses' station, getting so worked up that the entire ward can hear. "They control your every move in here," he complains. "You can't shit or piss or puke without them telling you how to do it! And they don't give a shit, they're robots. And I get held down and they stick needles in me!"

He hangs up and paces the ward, agitated. "Fucking robots! They're like Nazis, aren't they?" He asks no one in particular, he's just trying to get the other patients riled up.

"Hey!" says a nurse. "That's enough, watch your language!" Other patients are getting worked up. Any kind of problem or disturbance on the ward and, more often than not, Brandon seems to be involved.

Shortly, Brandon is silent. I've noticed that when a patient has a meltdown, we often don't hear anything from them for hours afterward. I have my suspicions as to why.

I have been nothing but impressed with the hospital protection officers (HPOs) here. From what I have seen, every crisis is dealt with swiftly, safely and quietly, leaving the patient with as much dignity as possible while minimizing risk and discomfort to other patients and staff.

I stay in bed the entire afternoon. I don't have the energy to go out to the common area today. I do my homework though, reading articles on both things Doctor Lewis asked me to look up: the theory of radical acceptance and the family systems theory. It's interesting reading and takes me back to my days as a psychology student. I have always been fascinated by psychology; I wish I'd stuck with it and finished my degree.

Brett pops his head in a couple of times, but the awkwardness remains and he doesn't stay to talk.

I am relieved when, after dinner, Emily knocks softly on the frame of the open door. "Hey, can I come in to chat? How are you feeling tonight?" Once more, she asks the list of standard questions and laughs. "You know, I have patients that, as soon as they see me, they begin rattling off the answers to this list of questions they know I'm going to ask. How was your day today?"

"It was… well…" I shrug helplessly. "I'm sure you heard things got a bit tense in here this afternoon."

"Yeah," she sighs. "Honestly, things are usually a lot less chaotic here. It's just the mix of patients on the ward right now, and the challenges from COVID restrictions. And because the psychiatrists don't see all their patients on the weekends, we can't really move anyone."

She asks how my anxiety has been, and I tell her about my panic attack, and how, despite my best efforts, I could not manage to distract myself.

"Did you take anything?" she asks.

"No," I say, a little abashed. "I didn't see the nurse and I was way too anxious to leave my room to look for him. I thought I should just try and push through it anyways."

"It's okay to take meds," she says. "You're in the hospital, the doctor has prescribed them as needed, and we are dispensing them to you. They aren't being abused, and you aren't being graded, you don't lose marks because you ask for something to help you. Do you think it would be helpful if we make a note for the nurses to ask you more directly if you need anything when they check in on you?"

I agree.

"What else did you get up to today?" she asks.

"Not much, I read a lot. I didn't leave my room today," I say somewhat guiltily.

"That's totally okay," she says. "You had a really, really rough day yesterday."

I laugh, a little embarrassed.

"Is there anything in particular you want to talk about tonight?"

I pause to think. "Boundaries, I guess. Like what we were going to talk about in group yesterday before it all kind of went sideways."

"How do you feel about setting boundaries in your life?" she asks.

"I suck at it." I laugh. "I guess, growing up, I didn't really see a whole lot of healthy boundaries. As I've gotten older, some people seem to think that, because of my blindness, I should have different boundaries than other people. Like someone can come up behind me in public, grab me and start pulling me in a different direction, and I'm just supposed to accept it because they're only trying to help. Or some stranger on the bus thinks it's okay to ask about my medical history, and they get offended when I don't want to answer their questions."

She seems incensed. "Are you serious? I'm sorry people are like that. It's not okay. I've had my share of strangers ask me weird questions on the bus, and you're right. It's really hard to be firm when we are taught to be polite."

"Yeah, if you stand up for yourself, you're in the wrong for being a bitch to some poor soul who's just trying to get in their good deed for the day. If a stranger grabbed an able-bodied person, a negative reaction would be completely expected and acceptable."

"You're right," she says. "Perhaps a good goal for your time here would be to work on establishing firm boundaries with people, while you're in a safe and controlled environment."

She must see the skeptical look on my face, because she continues. "I should tell you this, because you might not be aware of it. But every time you are out of your room, in the activity room or whatever, there is an aide constantly monitoring every part of the common area. It's the policy here. They might not be speaking, but they are always watching. There are always nurses around too, and during the weekdays there are also doctors and higher-level nursing staff walking the halls. We also have a clear view of your room from the nurses' station and can see as soon as you step out the door. As well, there are some patients here who are flagged to have a dedicated care aide with them at all times when they are out of their rooms. You are safe here."

Now that I think about it, I realize the staff-to-patient ratio here is extremely high. Even when I'm in my room, I'd estimate that someone, either an aide, nurse or doctor, has eyes on me about once every minute during the day as they walk past and glance in through the doorway. Even so, I don't feel completely convinced. But she's right, I should work on establishing boundaries while here. It's a relatively forgiving environment, since everyone is working through something.

"How are you liking the Ensure®?" she asks, noticing the half-empty bottle from dinner on my tray table. I shrug and pull a face. "There's a reason they don't serve it in restaurants," she says wryly.

We chat for a while about books and music, sharing recommendations. I feel like she sees me as more than a totally crazy person in need of fixing. More than anyone here, she seems to understand and be interested in my identity outside of these walls.

Emily returns a short time later with evening meds. I am relieved when she tells me that Doctor Lewis re-prescribed the sleep med I was taking before I was admitted.

I lie back, feeling sleepy and relaxed. Sleep comes quickly and easily tonight.

Day Seven

I wake up early, feeling rested. The morning dizziness I've been experiencing from the new meds seems to be diminishing. Emily comes in for her last check before going off shift. She asks how my night was and says she'll see me this evening.

My breakfast arrives. There are two tiny sausages tucked in next to the soggy scrambled eggs on my tray. They must be going all out for Sunday morning breakfast. I eat the sausages, toast and plain oatmeal, but I can't stomach the eggs.

I'm relieved when my new nurse introduces himself. This one actually stays to chat for a few minutes and doesn't seem to be suppressing the urge to bolt from the room like the one yesterday. He reminds me there's a piano if I want to play. I guess he read my file.

After a while, all seems quiet, so I head down the hall to the nurses' station to get what I need for a shower. The nurse actually lets me have a disposable razor; I'm apparently moving up in this strange new world. He makes a note of it in a log book on the desk and says I will need to bring it back immediately after my shower. I can't get to my room without passing the nurses' station anyway, so I would have no way of absconding with it if I were so inclined.

I try to juggle everything in one hand while using my cane in the other; he comes out from behind the desk to help me and to unlock the shower. Thankfully, they have replenished their supply of women's shampoo.

After my shower, I stop at the nurses' station to drop off the razor and towel on my way back to my room. I sit on the edge of the bed, brushing my hair—now shoulder-length and brown instead of long and jet black—and trying to gather my courage to head out to the common area. Other than to shower, I haven't left my room since I returned from group two days ago. I still feel afraid. What if I run into Paul out there?

Before I can give it too much thought and talk myself out of it, I stand quickly and make my way to the door. I take a deep breath and dart across the hall to the activity room, where I perch on the edge of my usual chair, closest to the exit.

A younger guy is running on the treadmill in the mini exercise gym at the back of the room. A patient I vaguely recognize approaches him. "Hey, what are you in here for?" Treadmill Guy ignores him, so he repeats his question.

"Because I am." Treadmill Guy finally answers. "I've gotta go." He hops off the treadmill and begins using another piece of equipment, which allows him to turn his back to the other patient and put some distance between them.

I watch this exchange with interest. *Well played, dude, well played.* Good use of boundaries. If it were me, I probably would have told the guy my whole life story just to avoid conflict and be polite.

I sit there for as long as I can stand it, trying to slow my breathing, calm my racing heart, and keep my hands from shaking. Through the open door I hear Erin, one of the girls from group, playing piano. She's all right, and the familiarity of the sound calms me a little.

"I'd sure love to learn to play the piano," an older woman says wistfully when the song is done.

"I'd teach you," says Erin, "but it's really, really hard." I try not to roll my eyes. I almost offer to teach her a bit, since the only thing I have in here is time. Then I remember I'm doing my best not to talk to anyone, so I stay silent.

I hurry back to my room when I figure it's getting close to lunch; I've been out long enough for the staff to notice and be happy about it. The weekends are boring and unstructured. There is no group wellness or other activities. In non-COVID times, there would be visitors to break up the monotony, but visitors are currently barred to limit the spread of the virus, so no one comes.

I'm lonely. I wish I could see Jordan, my family and my closest friends in person, but there's another part of me that's glad they can't visit. Even if visitors were allowed, I probably would have asked them not to come. I don't want them to see me in this place, to hear the other patients, to think I must be truly crazy to have landed myself in here. I worry that the image of me in a hospital bed in the psych ward would stay with them long after I get out. In the long run, I decide it's better they aren't able to visit.

While I'm pondering the logistics of visitors to the psych ward, something occurs to me. If this were any other ward, our hospital rooms would probably be decorated with flowers, stuffed animals and 'get well soon' cards from loved ones or work colleagues. There is nothing like that here. Granted, bouquets would need to be in plastic vases and any gifts would be searched for dangerous objects. But, more than that, I suppose people still view the psych ward as something very different than going to the hospital for a physical illness. What exactly would someone write in a card about recovering mental and emotional stability?

At lunch, one of the aides gently chastises me for not eating enough. I'm just not hungry. We eat five times a day here: three meals and two snacks. It feels like all we ever do is eat and, coupled with anxiety, I often feel nauseated.

True to form, by afternoon, the patients begin to get restless and irritable. Commotion ensues. I hate to hear people yelling. I try to fight my oncoming panic attack with breathing exercises and distraction, but it hovers there, set to take over at any moment.

Someone walks in and I'm relieved. I'll ask them for a low dose of a sedative, just enough to take the edge off. "I'm one of the medical doctors here," he says in a strong British accent. He puts emphasis on the word 'medical' so I know he's not one of the psychiatrists. I'm disappointed, he's probably not someone I can ask for drugs.

"There were some slightly abnormal results on your ECG, so I wanted to stop by and check that everything's okay," he tells me. He holds my wrist for a moment. "Okay, you're fine," he says nonchalantly, then bustles out the door. I wonder if he felt my heart racing.

I am actually slightly concerned about said irregularities. If they had told me this a few days ago, it would have been welcome news indeed.

Patients continue to be unruly, and I am getting more and more anxious. My nurse pokes his head in and asks if I need anything.

"Umm, I'm feeling really anxious and I was wondering if I could get some Ativan," I say in a rush.

"No problem," he says moving into the room. "Want to tell me what's up?"

"I don't know, just all the people freaking out on the ward and also it seems like everyone here thinks I have an eating disorder so they're always telling me to eat more but really it's just a symptom of the reason I'm in here and I can't eat because my anxiety makes me feel nauseated all the time!" My words tumble out, and I barely take a breath.

"That's fair," he says sympathetically, and leaves to get the meds.

I let the tablet dissolve under my tongue and wait for the relief it will soon bring. As it starts to take effect, I feel a war raging within my body. Ativan belongs to the drug class of benzodiazepines, tranquilizers that work by depressing the central nervous system. Because my fight-or-flight response is so deeply ingrained from years of nearly constant anxiety, I feel my body trying to keep my heart rate accelerated, my breathing rapid and my muscles tensed, fighting the drug as it works to slow everything down.

Eventually, the drug wins the battle and my head and limbs become heavy. I lean back against the pillows and close my eyes. All the chaos seems so far away now. I let the feeling of utter peace wash over me. It feels so good—I don't want to sleep, I want to hold on to this as long as I can.

I lie there, drifting in and out, enveloped in a peaceful haze. I am unaware of the time passing. I realize I've fallen asleep when Emily walks into my room. Hours have gone by.

"Hey," I say sleepily. "I was just dozing."

"That seems like a great activity for a Sunday afternoon."

"I wish life could always feel like it does on Ativan," I sigh contentedly.

"Don't we all," she laughs. "How was your day?"

"Pretty good. I went out to the common area for a bit." I tell her about the interaction between Treadmill Guy and the patient who asked why he was there.

She laughs. "That's certainly one way of establishing boundaries."

"But then I got too anxious and I had to leave." I sigh. "I didn't talk to anyone. Then I came back here and after a bit I freaked out and had to ask for a sedative."

"I wonder if having you start by going out to the common area on a low dose of Ativan would help. That way you can get more comfortable without being completely overwhelmed by anxiety."

I nod in agreement.

"The doc stopped by earlier and chatted with you about the results of your ECG?" she asks.

"He came and took my pulse, but he didn't say much about what they found on the test, just that there were slight abnormalities."

"The abnormalities are really nothing to worry about. Lots of things can throw it off, like extreme stress."

I think back to the evening of my ECG, remembering how distraught I had been.

"Do you have any thoughts about going home?" she asks. "I mean, you haven't been here that long, but how does the thought of home make you feel?"

"Scared," I admit. "I think I'm kind of like an addict. Like when you put a recovering addict in a new environment and give them tools to manage their addiction. For some of them, the temptation to use will lessen. But some people, when they go back to the same place where they used before, or back to the same partner or group of friends or whatever, the temptation can be too much. I think dying by suicide, the thought of it, is kind of like my addiction. Here I don't think of it all

173

that much, because I'm in a different environment and I'm constantly being reminded of healthier coping skills. But when I go home, when I'm back in that environment with the same triggers, and without anyone reminding me of CBT twenty times a day, maybe the temptation will get stronger."

"That makes a lot of sense," she says thoughtfully. "And I appreciate your honesty in sharing. You're right, we often say in here that the real work starts when you go home, because you don't have those constant reminders."

She says she'll be back with night meds shortly, but I stop her at the door, remembering something. "I have a phone appointment with my regular therapist tomorrow. Should I keep it?" I ask.

"Yes, definitely. I'll make a note for Doctor Lewis to have him come see you later on his rounds, after you're finished your appointment."

"Will Chris, my therapist, know I'm in here? Can he see all that medical info?"

"He will know, and he can see some of it," she explains. "Patient records can be accessed throughout the whole of the health authority, but he won't be able to see the medical things, like test results. He'll see our progress reports though, and we can see his. There's an advantage to having been hospitalized, actually. That will be in your records, and you'll be fast-tracked for any psych supports you need in the future."

"Hmm," I muse. "That doesn't really seem fair to all the other patients waiting. I was supposed to see a psychiatrist on an urgent basis, and that was booked in May for the middle of July. It's a shame it has to come to this for patients to receive quicker mental health support."

She sighs. "Preach sister, preach! I don't think there's a single psych nurse in here who wouldn't agree."

She leaves, then returns a few minutes later with night meds. She tells me she'll check in after she finishes with some other patients, and we can chat more if I'm still awake.

We never do have that chat. I fall asleep almost instantly.

Day Eight

I wake up later than usual. I was hoping to catch Emily before she went off shift to thank her, but she has already left. I'm starting to sleep well. I'm no longer aware of the nurses, who still shine their flashlight on me every fifteen minutes during the night.

I am, however, dismayed to discover that Brandon has managed to get a guitar in here. It doesn't seem like a particularly safe item to have in the psych ward, but I suppose they will keep it in lockup when he's not using it.

He's in fine spirits, strumming the same combination of notes, that do not make up a chord, over and over again on the painfully out-of-tune instrument. "Peace and love, brother!" he enthusiastically greets another patient walking by.

I hurriedly eat breakfast and grab my phone, waiting for Chris to call.

"Hey," he says when I pick up, "I hear you've had a change in location. I'm sorry. How are you?"

"I'm okay, you know, discounting the fact that I'm locked up in a psych ward." I laugh a little.

"What brought you there?" he asks, and I summarize the events of the past weeks. "Well, I'm glad you had the courage to go. How are you feeling about things?"

"Okay. I understand why the doctors kept me here. And I'm starting to realize that it's not so much that I want to die, I guess it's more that I don't want to live like this anymore." I hadn't planned to tell him that, but as I say it, I realize it's true. Death is appealing simply because it will put an end to the way I feel. Almost every waking moment of every day, I am afraid.

"Ah, now we're getting somewhere!" he exclaims. "I hope you know how truly resilient you are. You've fought this for so long, and you're still here fighting. That says something about your strength. And the fact that you, only now, ended up in hospital… Please don't think that ending up in hospital means you're weak. Even if you have to go back every once in a while, that's not weakness, it's bravery. It shows you believe you're worth fighting for."

I've been hearing variants of this a lot since I came here. I'm not sure if I'm strong, and I'm not even sure I'm worth fighting for. But I'm at least going to try.

"How is your anxiety in there?"

"Not great, I get anxious when the shit hits the fan with other patients. And psych emergency was definitely an experience. Have you ever had to work in there?"

"Yes, I have," he says knowingly. "What do you do when shit is hitting the fan?"

"I do breathing exercises, we've been working on meditation, and they had me make a list of things I can do to distract myself when I start feeling anxious. It often doesn't work though," I admit.

"Just like anything, it takes a lot of practice. It's not easy, but you're taking big steps. I'm sorry you're in the hospital, I know it's not fun. But I'm also glad you're there."

"It was in my safety plan," I say, referring to the document we wrote together when I first started sessions with him. It lists signs to watch for when I'm first beginning to spiral, and spells out the steps I should take when things get bad. The very last step on the plan, after all else fails: Go to the hospital.

"I guess I kind of felt that writing it was some sort of promise, and I didn't want to die with a broken promise," I tell him.

When I hang up, I head to the activity room. It's still early, and my hope is that there won't be anyone there. I sit in my usual spot by the door, and as far as I can tell, there is only one other patient in here, an older man who is flipping through channels on the TV.

To my dismay, he rises from his chair and comes over. I remember him; he's the patient who was talking to Treadmill Dude the other day. "Oh, sweetie," he says sadly. "What are you doing in here?"

My mind races. At first I think he's asking why I'm in this room, before I realize he's referring to the ward. I think of Emily and our conversations around setting boundaries. "The doctors say I need to be," I say dismissively.

"But why?"

"Because they say so," I answer.

He gets bored with me and goes back to watching TV. Not perfect establishing of boundaries, but better than I'd normally do. Maybe I can carry this forward to when people ask me rude, invasive questions out in public.

I feel my anxiety mounting; what if he wants to talk more? So, I get up and head to my room. On the way, I pass a confused patient trying to leave through the locked doors of the ward. When a nurse asks what she's doing, she says she's going home.

"You can't go home," the nurse says kindly but firmly. "You're in the hospital."

"Yes, I can," the patient retorts.

"You'll have to talk to your doctor about that," the nurse says, knowing she won't win this battle. It's hard to watch confused patients try to leave. It must be scary for them, not knowing where they are and why they can't go home.

No sooner do I get back to my room, when Marisol comes and asks if I want to sit in the solarium. I think she's making it her personal mission to get me out more.

The heat in the tiny solarium is stifling, the midday sun beating down on its glass roof and walls. The fertilizer they're using on the plants smells like shit. At least I hope it's fertilizer... One never can be too sure in here.

I've only been here a minute when Doctor Lewis walks in. There is one other patient in the room, and he asks her if she would mind stepping out so he can chat with me in private. She grumbles, but gets up and leaves.

I feel guilty for inconveniencing her; I suppose Doctor Lewis did it because he knows the herculean effort it will take for me to leave my room once I'm back there.

"How was your weekend? Did the nurses do therapy with you?" I tell him they did, a lot. He is pleased. He is even more pleased, and slightly surprised, when I tell him I'd been reading about the family systems theory.

"What do you think of it?" he asks.

"I think I have a new excuse for when people ask why I'm not having kids." I laugh.

"So, family sucks sometimes?"

I shrug. "I guess you could say that."

Basically, the family systems theory views family members as deeply interconnected emotionally, a cohesive unit rather than a group of individuals. The members of the family unit react to the perceived needs, emotions and difficulties of each other member. This leads to interdependence, which is more prevalent in some families than in others, but always present to some degree.

"Let's talk about that inner five-year-old you mentioned the other day. As an adult now, what would you say to that little girl, the first time her father left?"

My mind travels back through the years. I am sitting on the floor of my bedroom, and my parents are fighting again. I do my best to ignore it; I tell myself that they're adults, they'll make everything okay in the end.

But, then there is a duffel bag and I'm crying. Dad is leaving, and I'm begging him not to.

After a time, he relents. He says he just can't do it. I'm relieved, and ask him again, just to make absolutely sure. I fall asleep, contented. Safe.

But upon waking, the house is cold and dark, with none of the usual sounds of my father getting ready for work.

He is gone.

When I get off the school bus later that afternoon, he is still not back, but my grandparents have made the three-hour trip to be here with my mother, brother and me. My grandma enfolds me in her soft embrace that always smells of baking and talcum powder. When I ask her about my dad, she tells me he's not there because he's a little sick right now. I'm confused. Sick how? Did the cancer come back?

Back in the present, I pause to think. "I'd like to tell my younger self everything will be okay, but that would be a lie. So, I guess I'd just tell her the honest truth."

"Yes," Doctor Lewis agrees. "Parents should be the strong ones, and tell their children what's going on even if it hurts. A healthier response would have been to tell you that your dad was going to leave, before he left, but that he would still see you, and that he loves you. Those aren't easy things for most adults to say though, so it was easier to just gloss over the truth.

"Do you know about the five primal fears?" he asks. I shake my head so he begins listing them: "The fear of ceasing to exist, total annihilation. The fear of bodily mutilation or invasion, of having physical boundaries invaded, feeling unsafe or under attack. The fear of loss of autonomy, a lack of control. The fear of abandonment or rejection. The fear of humiliation.

"These are present in all of us to some extent. But, in some people, certain events can cause these fears to become crippling and interfere with daily life.

"Do you feel anxious right now?" he asks.

"Yeah."

"Which of these fears do you think is driving your anxiety in this moment?"

"The fear of humiliation," I answer.

"Why is that?"

"Because I'm out here in the common area, and I'm afraid I might do something stupid because then, what will people think? And even in this conversation, I'm afraid of saying something dumb, of being wrong about something, or not giving you an answer you'll like, because then you'll think I'm stupid."

"Makes sense," he says. "The good news is that most of these fears are very treatable with psychotherapy. The hardest to treat is the fear of non-existence; we usually see that as a problem for people who have suffered severe neglect in infancy."

"I'd say that's the least of my fears."

"Any others you feel cause you great difficulty in your life?"

"The fear of being unsafe, lack of control, and of being abandoned."

"Yes, these are all things that have come up during our sessions. But I think you're on a good path, and you have some good tools now. You've worked hard on coping strategies with the nurses, you have a good therapeutic relationship with Chris, you know he isn't going to abandon you, and that it's a safe environment. You have a psychiatrist now. I believe the acute phase has passed. Have you talked to your partner at all about going home? What are his feelings?"

"Yeah, I think he'd like me to come home, but he also wants me to do whatever is necessary to get better."

"I had a meeting with the nurses. We were talking about discharging you today, but I think I'd like to keep you in here one more day so you can get used to the idea of going home and put everything in place. I haven't heard back from the specialist about your genetic test results, so I'd like to try and get those today as well.

"We'll chat more tomorrow and see how you're feeling about things," he says, as he stands and opens the glass door of the solarium.

I'm surprised, the nurses never gave any indication of when I'd get to go home. I am okay with spending another night; the thought of walking out at this moment is terrifying. How odd that this place has come to signify safety.

Lunch will arrive soon, so I head back to my room. I think this may be my last lunch here and am relieved. I marvel at how they always manage to make the soup taste the same, although it appears to have different unappetizing things floating in it each day.

My nurse for the day, Melissa, walks in while I'm eating, and asks me the usual questions.

"The doctor said I'm probably going home tomorrow," I tell her.

"Really? How are you feeling about that?"

"Scared," I say honestly.

"Yeah, it's a big step," she says sympathetically. "But the doc wouldn't send you home if he didn't think you were ready."

I hope she's right.

"Hey, has anyone talked to you about rooms yet?" she asks. I have no idea what she's talking about. "Unfortunately, we have to move you. There's a patient coming back from rehab, and we need this room to be able to monitor him. Really sorry to have to uproot you. If you can pack up, someone will come get you when your room's ready."

She leaves and I begin to gather my things. All of a sudden, I wish I were going home today, since things are changing anyway. What if I end up with a roommate?

Christina knocks on the door and asks if I want to go to group. I shock myself by agreeing, both because I've heard Paul isn't going and because I clearly enjoy punishing myself. Then, Marisol comes and asks if I want to go back out to the solarium. I tell her I need to wait until they come get me to switch rooms. I don't trust anyone else to bring all my things over. I'm starting to get overwhelmed.

When Christina comes back to say group is starting soon, I am still waiting to be moved. I tell her I can't make it. She says we can try again on Wednesday, and I don't mention that I probably won't be here.

I sit and wait, listening to Brandon parade up and down the hall with his guitar. He still hasn't tuned it and he still isn't playing actual chords. "It's gonna be a good day today, nobody's gonna die today." He strums with great enthusiasm and sings joyously, but tunelessly.

That might not be true if you keep this up, I think wryly. I suddenly realize my hands are aching to play his guitar. It has been such a long time since I've wanted to have anything to do with music.

Finally, Melissa comes and helps me carry my things to my new room. It's a double, but the other bed is mercifully empty.

"Sorry about having to move you," she says, "but there's no one else in here and we're going to do our best to keep it that way."

I sit there, feeling anxious, as the afternoon unruliness takes hold of the ward. Today is particularly bad.

Brandon is yelling at an aide who won't let him wash a single pair of socks in the washing machine. "Fine! I'm just going to throw them in the garbage then. What a fucking waste!" Try as she might, the aide cannot convince him to hold on to them until he has more clothes to wash. I never do hear what happens to the socks.

Another patient—a usually benevolent, albeit confused, man—is uncharacteristically noncompliant, refusing necessary medical treatment. There's another patient whom they can't wake up, and tensions mount until he finally stirs.

A nurse comes running down the hall toward the nurses' station. "Call security," she says calmly but urgently. A code white is called over the PA system. During my time here, I have learned that code white signifies a violent, out-of-control person. Shortly, I hear that a patient is going to be transferred to the PICU.

As the supper trays arrive, I overhear one aide confide to another that it's her first day here and she's scared. She sounds frazzled. Her first shift has definitely been a baptism by fire. When she comes into my room, I try hard to be extra nice, because I know some patients won't be. I am reminded of the young male nurse on Saturday, and it makes me sad to know that some of the less-experienced psych workers have been scared of me, simply because I'm here. Contrary to what books and media would have you believe, we aren't all crazed animals. There are many people in psych wards like me, who quietly keep their heads down and work hard to get better and go home.

I'm halfway through dinner when a nurse I haven't met comes in and asks for the name of my nurse. I tell him and he exclaims that I have a good memory, much in the way one would speak to a two-year-old who remembered all her letters. "You're getting a roommate," he announces cheerfully.

Oh shit. I cannot muster up a single ounce of enthusiasm for his news.

After dinner, I call Jordan. "Shit! I'm getting a roommate!" I exclaim, as soon as he picks up. "What if she's like, a psycho killer or something?"

"That sucks," he says. "Maybe she'll be nice."

"Maybe…" I say dubiously. "I talked to the psychiatrist today, he says I can probably come home tomorrow."

"Really? That's awesome!" he says. "How are you feeling about it?"

"Kind of scared. It seems a bit sudden. But I've had some time to think about it this afternoon, and I think I'm ready."

"Just let me know what time you're getting discharged, and I'll be there to pick you up."

I wait for the mysterious new roommate, but nobody comes. Maybe the other nurse was mistaken; they don't seem to do many patient transfers after dinner. Maybe my nurse told him to find somewhere else for the new arrival. Just as I'm starting to relax, they walk in.

The nurse is followed by a patient I instantly recognize. She's the woman from the first night who was taken to the little padded room after saying she sometimes wants to be violent. I can almost hear the universe laughing. Is this one final test of my sanity? My anxiety is through the roof, and I want to ask for drugs, but then I worry they'll decide I'm not ready to go home. Patients have usually been somewhat stabilized by the time they arrive on this ward, so I tell myself it'll be fine.

The patient, Patty, is greeting the staff like they're old friends. She has clearly been here before.

In her lucid moments, Patty is a kind-hearted, interesting woman. We discover that we both love to travel, and we begin sharing stories of our adventures. She tells me that she worked in healthcare in her former life. "I could never be a psych nurse," she confides, "they have to put up with way too much shit."

It takes a special type to be a psychiatric nurse, tough as nails one minute while dealing with an unruly patient in the midst of a psychotic break, then brimming with compassion the next. Staff on psych wards are extremely underappreciated for all they have to do. They are the ones who deal with people no one else wants to, those who have hit rock bottom, the people that the rest of society fear, casting them aside as crazy.

In her confused moments, Patty struggles. She scratches at her skin, mumbling syllables that do not seem to make words.

My night nurse, Angie, comes in while Patty is out of the room. She's a tiny wisp of a girl who seems impossibly young. Angie is vaguely familiar to me, and I wonder if she was my nurse on the night I was sedated. If so, she makes no mention of us having met before.

"I see you got a roommate," she says conspiratorially. "That's always a bit annoying." I'm surprised when she lets me have a cable so I can charge my bluetooth headphones. I think I'm going to need them tonight. I guess she figures it's safe, that I'm not about to hang myself, since I'm well enough to potentially go home tomorrow.

To my annoyance, I realize I left my hospital socks and pyjamas in my old room, so I head out to the nurses' station to ask for new ones. I couldn't have picked a worse time. They're going to be showing a movie in the activity room, and a nurse is making popcorn. Patients crowd around, waiting anxiously for a treat we don't normally get in here.

"Hey, blind girl," calls a guy standing in front of the desk. "What's your name?"

I tell him, and he says his name is Adrian. He is awkward and gawky, not quite grown into himself yet, barely more than a kid really.

"Why is the tip on your cane so small?" he asks. "There's another guy in here with a cane, and his is giant."

"You mean Adam?" Brandon asks. "He left this morning."

Two blindies on the same psych ward, what are the chances?

"Umm, it's personal preference, I guess." I shrug. Small talk on the psych ward, there's never a dull moment.

A middle-aged woman sits in a chair across from the nurses' station, making a fuss because she apparently wasn't read her rights under the Mental Health Act within the requisite 48 hours. She says she plans to take it up in a hearing with the review panel. Other patients are sympathizing with her. I'm not. Yes, perhaps there was an oversight, but the nurses in here are doing everything they can, working under the extra burden of the additional precautions put in place because of COVID-19. Would things truly have been that drastically different if she was read her rights a few hours earlier?

At long last, a nurse notices me waiting and, having gotten what I came for, I make my escape down the hall.

I ask for night meds early, the sooner I sleep, the sooner this will be over. I pray they'll let me go home tomorrow. Having a roommate is less than ideal.

I somehow drift off, even while listening to Patty scratch violently and mumble things I don't understand.

Day Nine

I sleep poorly. The mattress is uncomfortably thin and its vinyl cover crinkles whenever I move, Patty snores and calls out to God in her sleep, and there was a code blue in the middle of the night. It's not even light out when a nurse I don't recognize greets me on one of her checks. "You're awake, how was your night?"

"Oh, you know," I say, shrugging and casting a glance toward the curtain that divides the room in half.

"Ah, yeah," she says knowingly.

The breakfast trays come and Patty is still asleep. She was up late last night.

I'm halfway through breakfast, still in hospital pyjamas, when Doctor Lewis walks in. I'm surprised, I've never seen him this early. "How are you feeling?" he asks.

I tell him I'm fine, and he asks if I've had any thoughts since yesterday that I'd like to share.

"You know," I say, "I think if someone can really start to heal in this place, they're a lot more resilient than they think. They can continue getting better anywhere."

"Very true. Do you have everything in place to go home today?" He asks. I nod.

"Great, you'll be discharged at some point today, and the nurse will schedule an appointment for you to see me in a week for any medication adjustments. I still haven't been able to make contact with the specialist for your genetic test results, but I'll give him one more call this morning." I'm grateful to him for trying.

"You've worked really hard," he tells me. I find it a little funny, I've barely moved from my hospital bed since I got here, but I know what he means.

Time passes. Patty wakes up and we chat idly. I listen sadly while a patient tries to schedule out-patient counselling services and is told there's a wait of several months. A younger patient is on the phone, trying in vain to find supportive housing so he won't end up back on the street when he's discharged. We are told to trust in the system, but I think the system has failed all of us in here, to one degree or another.

I schedule a time for my discharge with one of the nurses, and call Jordan to make the necessary arrangements.

Finally, an older nurse I don't know comes in with a bunch of paperwork. She gives me a list of prescribed medications and nutritional supplements. There is also a long list of medical and psych appointments I need to attend, that I'm sure must rival Paris Hilton's social calendar. Unfortunately, she informs me, they still have not managed to make contact with the specialist, so I won't get my test results before I leave.

The nurse tells me that she'll be in a meeting but, when the time comes for my discharge, one of the mental health workers will escort me to the hospital's main entrance. I wish Emily were here. I would have liked to thank her and say goodbye.

I organize my things, though I haven't unpacked much since switching rooms. I find the T-shirt Morgan gave me back in PES, which seems like a lifetime ago. I bundle it in with the rest of my clothes. It's the one thing I'll take with me from this place, a reminder of where I've been and how far I've come.

Waiting impatiently, I watch the minutes crawl by on my phone's clock. My discharge time comes, then passes.

When I can stand it no longer, I decide to head out to wait by the nurses' station. "It was nice meeting you," says Patty. I tell her likewise, and I mean it. "Good luck," she says, her voice brimming with sincerity. "Don't come back here!" I smile and tell her I don't plan on it.

As I walk down the hall with my bag, nurses and care aides wish me well. "Good luck," they say. I notice they avoid telling me not to come back, probably so I'm not discouraged from seeking hospitalization again should I ever need it.

I wait in the exact spot where I had sat in my wheelchair when Morgan brought me down here. There is some confusion about who is going to escort me out of the hospital and release me to a responsible adult. As I stand waiting with a small group of aides and nurses, Brandon hurries toward us.

"Hey guys, did you know that Obama is an alien and Hillary Clinton went to the moon in 1953?" We smile and nod. I take this as confirmation; it's definitely time for me to go home.

Eventually, a care aide says she'll accompany me out of the hospital. Leaving the psych ward is more anticlimactic than I had imagined. We stand at the locked door, the aide presses a button on the wall, and someone in the nurses' station unlocks it. The door glides open with a tiny click and a soft, mechanical hiss, the only things that mark my return to freedom.

We walk through a maze of hallways in the main part of the hospital until we reach the entrance. I push open the door, inhaling deeply the sweet, fresh air I haven't breathed in what seems like such a very, very long time. Then I walk through the open door, and out into a warm, cleansing spring rain.

Homecoming

I stand in the hospital parking lot, clinging to Jordan as though I were drowning. I realize that, apart from medical procedures, it is the first physical contact I've had since I was admitted. Being without my loved ones for a short time has been desperately lonesome, I can't imagine how the patients in long-term care facilities must feel, locked inside for months with no visitors due to COVID-19. It is no life for anyone.

"You smell like the hospital," Jordan says. That smell has become something I no longer even notice.

In the car, we are both tentative. Neither of us quite know what to say. I ask how things have been going with our business since I've been away. Jordan asks if I'm hungry, and if I want to stop at the pharmacy to fill my prescriptions before we go home. I feel dazed, and I struggle to remember important things that have happened in the past several weeks. Just in time, I stop myself from asking about the health of Jordan's ailing grandfather, as I remember he passed away almost a month ago. How had I forgotten something so important? I feel like an insensitive asshole.

We arrive home and I curl up in bed with a book, exhausted from the excitement of my homecoming, and the lack of sleep the previous night. We order takeout from a local burger place. I think Jordan is surprised to see me eat. I fall asleep early, it feels so good to be back in my own bed.

The next morning, Doctor Austin calls, his clinic having been notified of my discharge. "I've been reading *all* your reports from the hospital." He puts emphasis on the 'all' and sounds tired, maybe a little sad. He asks what happened, and I repeat the story yet again.

"I'm glad they were able to give you some good support. Remember to communicate openly with the psychiatrists, don't tell them you're fine if you're not. They can really help you with medication adjustments."

The following week, Doctor Lewis' office calls and asks me to complete a TeleSage assessment—an online diagnostic test that screens for various psychiatric disorders. I find it odd since Doctor Lewis is already familiar with my case, but I figure they want the results on file, so I complete the self-assessment of a few hundred questions.

The next day the office calls back, saying Doctor Lewis won't be able to make our scheduled appointment, but that another doctor will meet with me via videoconferencing. This doctor turns out to be a regular family practitioner with no additional psych training. He explains to me that, because of COVID, the process has changed. Patients will now meet with a family physician, who will then confer with the psychiatrist on the patient's behalf, then generate a report that will be sent to the patient's own family doctor. The patient will need to make an appointment with their doctor to find out the results of the report. Only a government could come up with something so stunningly idiotic.

We discuss my entire history for an hour, and I have to keep repeating things Doctor Lewis already knew. It is distressing. The call keeps dropping and ends up being entirely unproductive and frustrating.

HEALING AT HOME

The first weeks after coming home, I am so very tired. Even climbing the stairs in my house is exhausting. It is odd to see the evidence of my life from the few weeks before my hospitalization, so many things I did of which I have no clear recollection. My therapists believe I spent most of that time in a dissociative state, my mind's way of protecting me from the trauma of what I was planning. It takes a few weeks for me to be able to find the courage to open my computer and see what I had left waiting to be found after my death. It isn't as painful as I thought it would be. I see my home through different eyes now: a warm, inviting, beautiful sanctuary, instead of the dark prison in which I had planned to die.

I have been keeping up with my many medical and mental health appointments, and they say I'm doing well enough that I don't need to check in quite so regularly. I suspect I may always need some degree of mental health support. My therapists feel I'm ready to try group therapy, in a much more targeted and controlled way than in the hospital, so I'm on the six-month waiting list for a group that meets to discuss the specific mental health challenges I face.

We have found a combination of medications that seem to be working well, although I still have occasional dizziness and tremors, side effects that will probably not go away. I may need to be on medication for the rest of my life, and I think I've made my peace with that.

I have recently been able to reconnect with some estranged family members. Truths were spoken—things left unsaid for over half my lifetime.

The longer I've been home, the more challenging certain things have become. As I suspected, obstacles felt a lot more manageable when the voices of the psychiatrists and nurses were fresh in my mind, reminding me of healthier habits. As time has passed, I've needed to make a conscious effort to not fall back into old patterns. Some days I am more successful than others.

On the bad days, I still find myself retreating. There are very few people I feel I can talk to when I'm not doing well, because they'll start to worry. They may even view my behaviour as a failure of my hospital stay to 'fix' me. Family and friends often treat my hospitalization as though I went in for some routine surgery or to repair a broken arm. "You're okay now, right?" They say it more as a statement than a question they don't want to hear the answer to. I tell them I am, just to reassure them. What they really mean is, "Please tell me you're all better because I can't stand to hear otherwise."

I have finally received the results of my genetic testing. While they were able to identify the gene responsible for my blindness, it isn't the one that can be addressed with the current available treatment. However, treatment for this one has reached human trials. In the next number of years, I will possibly need to make the decision of whether or not to pursue treatment to restore my sight.

With a nutritional plan and supplements, the effects of malnutrition and dehydration have begun to fade. I'm starting to feel stronger and less fatigued.

The uncertainty caused by the COVID-19 pandemic still weighs heavily on me, as it does for most. I still have dark days and dark thoughts, but they no longer consume my every waking moment. It's the oddest thing that on the hardest days, I crave the safe, understanding environment of the hospital, the place where I never had to pretend to be okay.

It's a funny thing, we go to the hospital to heal, but we come out with other traumas, things seen and heard that we will carry with us forever. The smallest things can bring me back to that time: a song, a smell or even a word spoken in a specific way. I still can't pass the hospital in the car without feeling a tightening in my chest. I have dreams that I end up back in the psych ward, or about things that happened while I was there. Sometimes it's a lonely feeling, an experience my loved ones, God willing, can never share with me. It is, without a doubt, one of the most difficult things I have ever been through. And yet, when I look back on it, I can only feel gratitude for the nurses and doctors, the care aides and even the other patients. Through them, I gained the tools and the strength to help myself.

EPILOGUE: AUGUST 2020

The sea in the bay is as smooth as glass, reflecting the vibrant colours of the setting sun. The heat of the day remains, even into this twilight hour. I take the clean, ocean air deep into my lungs, and my toes grip the stand-up paddle board as I glide across the water's surface. Back on the beach are gathered some of the people I love most in this world.

As in other moments during the two months since coming home from the hospital, I can't help but think to myself, I would have missed this. There are so many things I would have denied myself, had that kind emergency doctor made a different decision that day.

I dip my paddle rhythmically into the water, lost in thought. I don't know what comes next for me. Who knows, maybe I'll finally finish my psychology degree. Maybe I'll find a way to go live outside of Canada again. Or perhaps I'll translate these experiences into songs and release some new music. The important thing is that now, there are moments in which I am able to think of the future, something I hadn't been able to do for a long time. In the darkest times, I couldn't even think about the next day, because it took everything I had to just make it through the current one. I had no hope for the future.

For now, I'm taking one day at a time, always conscious of the fragility of my situation. I know that recovery is not going to be a linear process, and I know I may stumble and fall. My loved ones and I are now more aware of the signs that I am spiralling; but I will fight to keep my head above water, to never return to such a dark, hopeless place.

I know I'm one of the lucky ones. I have been able to afford interim private therapy while waiting for publicly funded mental health support. I have a doctor who takes my mental health concerns seriously, and a small group of loved ones who have supported me on this long and difficult journey, people whom I can talk to without the stigma and shame that is all too often associated with mental illness. And, when I needed to be, I was admitted into inpatient care in a hospital with a strong, holistically oriented psychiatric program.

Sadly, many are not so lucky. Too many people struggle alone because they are unable to access psychiatric support. Or, when help finally comes, from a government that views physical and mental healthcare as completely different entities, it is too late. When I think back to the two-month wait to meet with a psychiatrist on an "emergency" basis, it is clear to me that our healthcare system does not view serious mental health conditions as the acute, life-and-death crises they often are. People battling mental illness are too frequently afraid to speak out due to feared or previously experienced negative reactions from others.

We are not, nor should we try to be, professionals in the context of dealing with a loved one's mental illness; however, I believe it's crucial we learn how to speak about suicide and mental illness—about what responses are helpful in a mental health crisis, and what does more harm than good. We must, of course, also take care of our own needs to be able to support a loved one. Remember that, as with any other illness, you can't make them better. All you can do is be there and love them through it.

There is much work still to be done to end the stigma that surrounds suicide. We only need look at the language still used when discussing suicide and mental illness to know we have a long way to go in being able to speak openly about it. The common phrase 'to commit suicide' brings to mind an illegal or sinful act, instead of the tragic loss of life that comes from losing the battle with a life-threatening disease. When was the last time you heard of someone who committed a heart attack? When a person dies by suicide, it is the sad end to an illness as real as any other. If we begin to use more compassionate words, then maybe we can strip away the guilt and shame that causes so many to stay silent in their pain.

So, the next time you hear of someone who has died by suicide, I ask you to please react with compassion. If you are tempted to say, "I don't understand how they could be so selfish" or "Why did they take the easy way out?" please, instead, be grateful that you cannot understand the tortured mind of a person who feels they have no other option. And as for it being the easy way out? Let me assure you, there is nothing easy about being in that much pain.

And on the other side, if you have truly come to the end of the road, and you will know it unmistakably if you do, I stand with you in your pain, dear one. I won't tell you that it will get better, or that you matter. These are empty platitudes when you're in the thick of it, much as saying "I'm sorry" to someone who has lost a loved one. But know this: There is one final decision you must make and, either way, it will take all the strength you have left.

You are precariously perched on a thin wire; underneath you there is only darkness. Your way forward is blocked by an impenetrable wall. Eventually, you will fall, or jump, from the wire. You can't stay here long. But you have a choice. If you fall to the left, you will make a possibly irrevocable decision that, rest assured, will be devastating to someone, and it may not turn out as you hoped. The instinct for survival is strong—the body will fight long after the mind has given up.

Or, you can choose to jump to the right, and trust that, at the bottom of the dark and endless pit, there is someone waiting with a safety net to catch you.

AUTHOR'S NOTE

I knew I needed to tell this story as I lay awake in my hospital bed in a secure psychiatric ward. The idea for this book offered me the first tiny glimpse of a renewed will to live; the motivation to get well enough to leave the hospital, because I still had something I needed to do. As difficult as it has been to share my story, I could not keep silent; the social issues discussed in this book are rampant. Below are some sobering statistics that give us a clear snapshot of why these topics are so important to discuss:

- The most recent reports by the WHO (World Health Organization) estimate that, globally, one person dies by suicide every 40 seconds.

- Each year in Canada, one in five adults will experience a mental illness or addiction problem, according to The Centre for Addiction and Mental Health (CAMH).

- According to the Canadian Mental Health Association (CMHA), 49 percent of people in Canada who feel they have struggled with depression or anxiety have not discussed their concern with a doctor.

- In 2003/2004, 0.9 percent of Canadians were discharged at least once from an acute care hospital with a mental health diagnosis, according to Statistics Canada.
- 66 percent of working-age, visually impaired Canadians are unemployed, according to the Canadian National Institute for the Blind (CNIB).
- In a study comparing the rates of violence against women with and without disabilities, women with disabilities were found to be four times more likely to have experienced a sexual assault than their non-disabled counterparts.

While there is generally less stigma attached to both mental illness and disability than ever before, these numbers show that we still have a long way to go. My hope is that, through writing about these experiences, I can be a part of the voice that brings some clarity to the complex topics of mental illness and life as a person with a disability.

So often, when someone loses their battle with mental illness, the overriding question is, "Why? How could this happen?" Though our stories are all different, I believe there are some universal truths. I hope that, even in the smallest of ways, I can provide insight into this impossible question.

Although my experiences and opinions do not reflect those of all people who are blind, I think most of us would agree that doubts about our abilities have been a barrier at some point in our lives. I believe it's easier to look at us and feel pity, contemplating the visual things we miss—such as the blue of the ocean or our loved ones' faces—because it's something people can think about without feeling pressure to change their own beliefs. Considering the life of a blind person in such abstract ways protects people from the discomfort of knowing that societal attitudes are actually the problem, and that they, themselves, can and should be the catalyst for change.

Making a difference may feel like an impossible uphill battle for one person, but together, we can do incredible things. People with disabilities need your help, because we can't do it alone.

By openly discussing these topics, we can end the stigma and fear attached to them and help people who are fighting these battles to get the help and support they need. There are actions we can take together to make a difference:

- Take a mental health first-aid course to better know how to assist someone in crisis. There are many courses available both in person and online.

- Be open to talking about the hard stuff. If you're concerned about someone, don't be shy to ask them directly if they're okay, and listen to their answer. It's okay to be direct; it is a myth that talking about suicide will increase the likelihood that someone will take their own life. If you are in a place in your own journey where you feel you can support them, help to find professional resources to assist. Better yet, ask them if they would like you to help them make contact with these resources. Access to mental health support is not always easy, and the very nature of some mental illnesses makes it near impossible for a person to keep reaching out for support. How does one advocate for themselves again and again when they don't feel they're worthy of help?

- Contact your government to advocate for better mental health support. Government programs must become easier to access. Wait times of months, as in my story, for outpatient mental health support, can be extremely dangerous. People need access to individual support, medication and programs before it's too late.

- Treat people with disabilities the same as you would treat any other person, without talking down to them or believing you know what their lives are like due to your own biases. If you have the opportunity to hire a qualified person with a disability, take it. People with disabilities can be an excellent asset to a company, as many are extremely adept at problem solving, due to years of navigating a world that has not been designed for them.

Although the actions of some of the people in this book affect me to this day, I have made peace with the individuals themselves. I've learned that my anger will do nothing to affect those who have hurt me, but by living with hate toward them I only hurt myself. I believe that true evil is rare; people are inherently good but can do terrible things. We are all wounded, trying to deal with our demons in the best way we know how.

As honest as I've tried to be in recounting my story, there are some details I have intentionally left out or altered slightly, both for the safety of readers who are struggling with their own mental health, and the privacy of those whose lives have intersected with mine. In some therapy sessions shared, I have omitted details in order to preserve someone's anonymity. I have intentionally left out the specific mental illness discussed with Doctor Lewis for the privacy of my family members, as it carries a genetic component. On careful consideration, I felt that omitting this detail did not alter the essence of the story. In most cases, I do not mention medications by name, due to the individualistic, trial and error nature of the treatment. While I did discuss various methods of suicide, because I felt the book should not gloss over these hard truths, I omitted specific information for the well-being of any readers who may be struggling with suicidal thoughts. These acts are in no way recommended nor encouraged. If you find yourself contemplating suicide, please talk to a professional or someone you trust who can help you connect with the support you need. Please refer to the resources on the following page.

Whether you are struggling with your mental health, or you have lost a loved one to mental illness, whether you are a minority member fighting what feels like a losing battle with discrimination, or you are watching someone you love struggle with these issues, you are not alone.

MENTAL HEALTH RESOURCES

If you or a loved one is in crisis, there are places to turn for help:

Canada Suicide Prevention Service: 1-833-456-4566

National Suicide Prevention Lifeline (United States): 1-800-273-8255

Befrienders (Worldwide): http://befrienders.org

If you believe there is immediate risk, call 911 or go to the nearest emergency room

ACKNOWLEDGEMENTS

My most heartfelt thanks to the following people:

Jordan, for sitting with me in the darkest hours and loving me through it all.

My family, for being ready to lend support day or night and helping me find the courage to do what I needed to.

Chelsea and Eduardo, for being the greatest besties a girl could ask for and staying the course when things got tough.

Thanks also to:

The nurses and care aides in the hospital, for your incredible dedication and compassion. You aren't told "Thank you!" nearly enough.

The doctors and therapists who have worked with and supported me in and out of the hospital, providing me with such compassionate care through all the ups and downs.

The other patients in the hospital, many who helped me, sometimes in very difficult ways, to confront some things I needed to face. I wish each of you peace on your healing journey.

My fabulous editor Maraya, for helping me bring my story to life.

Jon, Jeff and everyone else who so willingly gave of their time and expertise.

Caroline, Lorraine, Beatrice, Brock, Mrs. Blerot and Mr. Wurtz, who always encouraged my creative endeavours.

To everyone I have been lucky to know through music, for your acceptance, for helping me feel a part of something so dear to my heart.

Manufactured by Amazon.ca
Bolton, ON